MAKING MOVES IN COLLEGE

By
JARED JONES

ISBN-13: 9780615901176
ISBN-10: 0615901174

STEP 1:

THE JOURNEY TO COLLEGE

Getting into college is a great aspiration for any person's to-do list, and it can definitely happen if you want it badly enough. There is always a way for anyone to get into college. Some people debate whether college is a necessary factor in today's society, while others feel that colleges are simply institutions that cause people to go into debt. However, the world around you works on investments—everyone eventually has to take a gamble to change things that put him or herself in a position to become more successful in life.

If you're reading this book, then your mind is either made up and you are going to college, or you are contemplating on whether to go to college. Either way, it is important to realize that the more you put into life, the more you get from life; so it's up to you if you want college to be a great investment for the rest of your life. Just saying "I'm going to college" is a great way to start out, but the actual steps to getting there are what can make or break your aspirations. In grade school, teachers prepare you by giving you what they perceive as the necessary fundamentals for getting you to the next grade; not to criticize grade school, but there should be a course in all said institutions to help students gain an insight on what they may want to do in life and to teach students about discovering their passions and handling adversity.

The feeling of wanting to go to college should be embraced by the student and not simply looked at as just the next step after high school graduation. When getting ready to look at colleges, it helps to have a good perception of where you want to be and what you want to do in the years after college. To those of you who don't really have a plan or idea of where you want to be, that is perfectly okay; but at the end of this book, you should have a firm focus and new outlook when it comes to pushing yourself every day of your life. With that said, we can now begin our journey to helping shape you into a more confident, successful, and knowledgeable individual.

In high school, I was told that I couldn't go to college because of my poor grades throughout my 12 years of grade school. I will admit, I had the "just do enough to get by" mentality. While I knew that I wanted to be successful, I didn't have any idea of how I was going to get there. My goal was just to graduate from high school and continue on to work, because that's what a lot of guys who went to my high school did. There were a lot of physical plants around my town and neighboring towns, and it was easy to make 12, 13, or even 14 dollars an hour by doing those physical labor-type jobs. When you're young and able to start making money right after high school, it's cool because it requires no extra schooling—all you need is to pass the company physical and drug test, and voila, you have a job. It was all about how fast the money could come to you and allow you to buy really nice things.

When I graduated from high school, I didn't know anything about writing business plans, investing my money, or setting up a retirement fund. I just knew that saving was very important and to spend my money wisely. The quickest way for me to obtain a reasonably decent amount of money was through the plant corporations. The only downside was that during the time I was finishing high school, those plants were laying people off, and I saw a lot of people who had spent years working at those plants fall into a depressed state, not knowing what to do next. At that time, I was 17 years old, and I knew that I didn't ever want to feel the way they felt, so I decided to establish some type of plan to succeed.

Now there are two things I want to state before I continue. First, I am a firm believer that your geographical location plays a small role in how successful you are. A lot of times when you're living in a rural town, it's easy to lose hope because of the lack of opportunities surrounding you. Secondly, the conditions surrounding myself made it obvious that I didn't want to be there—in no way am I criticizing anyone from wanting to work in factories. I understand that everyone's circumstances are different, but at a young age, I knew that any place would be better than where I was at that moment in my life. Now let's continue.

Having spent so many years in that small town, everyone told me to take any opportunity that I could and get out, because there was nothing back there to hold on to or stay for except for family. On the day that I graduated from high school, I just wanted to take a break; I had already been through 12 years of back-to-back schooling, so I was a little worn out.

During the summer after graduating from high school, people advised me to immediately continue my education with college, because it's hard to go back after putting it off—they were right. A week after graduation, I didn't know where to begin my life because everything seemed to move so quickly that I was overwhelmed with the many different paths in life. My experience in high school was easy because I followed a pre-established routine: wake up in the morning, eat breakfast, go to school, eat lunch, finish school for the day, and go home. It never occurred to me at that time that I would eventually have to break out of the mindset of having everything planned for me and start focusing on my future.

I was dependent on my parents to wake me up in the morning, make sure that I had everything I needed for school, and provide transportation for me—in other words, I was set. However, I didn't know what I wanted to do with my life in the long-term; all I knew was that I wanted to make a lot of money and be able to buy anything I desired. I lived in a small town in Georgia, so extravagant resources were harder to reach. To a lot of people in my town, Atlanta was considered "the big city." I had friends who felt the same way as me and just wanted to take a break after high school, but while it was easy for them to take a break from any kind of work, I realized that by doing nothing I would continue to be frustrated. I had a few other friends and family members who encouraged me to attend college and get a degree that would improve my chances of gaining employment in a career-oriented world. At the end of the day, though, I knew that it was my choice on whether to continue forward with my education or stay where I was and get a job. I will admit that my life was pretty secure because I had my parents to fall back on, but they were also the ones telling me that they wouldn't be there forever. I would say that their safety net did have a role in me being complacent. Realizing that one day that safety net would be gone and I could possibly end up being dependent on others and full of regret for not taking responsibility for my life was not what I wanted. My parents were established in their careers, my father was self-employed and my mother was a teacher so I had the ambition just not the drive yet.

As a kid, I daydreamed a lot about being able to see the world, travel, and be a respected businessman like my father, but the dreams would always end in frustration because I knew that I was a long way from that goal. In actuality, the fear of failure combined with self-doubt from having struggled in grade school was what really halted my ability to try new things early on. I would always say to myself, "Why try something, put all your energy into it, and still fall short?" At the time, you never really heard of too many people from my area going out, achieving success, and then coming back to share their journeys. To be even more honest, the fear deep inside me of the unknown also played a part in my decisions. The fact that I didn't know where I would be over the next couple of years was what scared me most.

My days were routine in grade school, and I had become complacent and satisfied with my position in life. What broke me out of that mindset was realizing that if I didn't at least take the chance at working toward having a future within my control, then I would be full of regret and never know what could have been. I also knew that I would be in the same position and possibly even worse as years passed—whether I thought I could do it or didn't think I could do it, I was right. After a few days of thinking, I came to the conclusion that where I was at that point in my life was not where I wanted to stay forever, so to put it simply, I knew that I had nothing to lose by giving college a try. Ultimately not wanting to remain in the same place for years to come brought the courage and drive that I needed. I had to change my thought patterns right then and there, because I needed nothing but positive energy around me to better my chances of succeeding. I started viewing everything around me as an opportunity waiting to be seized, and I decided that if I made a plan for myself and carried it out, then at least I could say I thought about every action I would take. I knew for a fact that it wouldn't hurt to have a college degree to fall back on, but the length of time that it would take to get one was a little discouraging. However, from hearing stories of successful people's failures, I knew that if the path to success came easily, then everybody would be successful, so I saw this as an opportunity to break out of my comfort zone and see where college would lead me.

I knew that I had to get out and establish myself, or I would be what they refer to in my hometown as stuck. My first step was to find colleges that would accept me, which proved to be hard because of the discouraged mentality that I had from my high school counselor telling me that my grades weren't good enough for college. Furthermore, my lack of focus in high school certainly didn't get me noticed by any colleges, and I knew that anywhere I went outside of my state and town would be expensive. Since my grades were low, I didn't have the opportunity to get scholarships to assist me financially while in college, so I had to make do with the resources that I had. I browsed different colleges, looking at all the fees and tuition money that it would cost me, and quickly realized that college was going to be very expensive. Even though my grades were low, there will still grants available to help me in college, but I wouldn't get any major full-ride scholarships. I also didn't play any sports in school, so I knew that the sports scholarships weren't attainable. However, I had the idea that college would be a fresh, new start for me, so I knew that I had to change.

A part of that change was facing one particular reason why I was indecisive about college. I was always concerned about having a huge amount of loans, because I knew of a lot of people with an extensive amount of debt attached to their name. However, I applied for and wrote essays for different scholarships and grants in hopes of getting a little money saved up to help me along the way, and it actually worked. I managed to save up enough money to pay for books and school supplies—the financial aid allowed me to avoid a huge amount of debt.

Before proceeding forward, I realized that in order to take even the first step toward going to college, I needed to get more focused. To get focused, I had to actually sit myself down, look at college from a broad perspective, and foresee where I wanted to go in my life. It was definitely a scary position to be in because at the time, the fear of failure was deeply rooted in me, and I had no idea of where and how to start and finish. To help combat that feeling whenever it arose, I would remind myself that taking a chance and failing at something was better than not taking the chance at all and never knowing what the outcome could be. Since I had the opportunity to outline my plan to get me to where I am today, I want to share with you what helped me by first helping you get focused.

A. GETTING FOCUSED

When I tell people to get focused, it is not to discredit any-body's intentions or current plans, because personal goals and plans are great. When I say "get focused," I mean for you to change your vision by looking at things as helping you in the long term, and to stand out in some way or fashion. Before continuing your education, you must realize that college is a competitive world. Your peers will compete for presidents of organizations, best fra-ternities or sororities, and, most importantly, careers. You have to examine what counts and what doesn't count in your personal plan—take steps forward and not backward.

To really get focused, it helps to educate yourself early on about different routes you can take for your career as well as the current state of careers around the world and the different roles they can play in your future. Doing this will get you in the habit of doing the research yourself before being asked to in college.

Getting into the habit of reading is fundamental and helps you grow mentally as a person. Not only does reading increase your intellect and vocabulary, but it helps you to better articulate what you want to say and how you want to say it. Also, don't limit yourself to just reading about various careers—any nonfiction and fiction material is great as well. Many answers you're search-ing for can be found in books, because somebody before you has likely already been in your position. Even though I was uncertain before college, I always read books which played a great role in strengthening my drive and helping me to overcome adversity.

Another task that will help your focus is to talk to people who have been in your position and get their take on their own col-lege experiences. This alone can sometimes be more helpful than any book or college commercial you may come into contact with. When conversing with them, find out what kept them motivated during harder times in college, how they overcame any struggles, and how college in general has played out for them.

It is important to keep in mind that you are not that person—in other words, whether their own experiences are negative or positive, you are still the captain of your future. It's up to you to steer your life in the direction that you want it to go. For example, I watched the news to see how the world was evolving around certain career markets and how people excelled in the profession I was interested in. I even talked to friends who dropped out of college as well as to some who graduated from college to get an overview of their college experiences. While some were helpful and others I felt didn't have my best interest at heart, at the end of the day, I knew that going to college was my choice and mine alone.

Now the next step to getting focused is to have a clear picture of how successful you want to be. I separate this into *present attainable* and *future attainable*.

The present attainable can be any short-term goal: getting all A's your first semester, making a specific number of friends, joining clubs that you're interested in. The future attainable, on the other hand, can be things like buying a house, traveling the world, or being a millionaire or billionaire of some sort. This will be part of the fuel that keeps you going when you get into college. Making a list of and reaching your future attainables is where everything you dreamed has the chance to come true, because you've seen yourself living that dream earlier on—now it's time to claim what's yours.

Personally, when I was at this point, I became obsessed with both the present and future attainable. I replayed them in my mind every morning when I woke up and again before going to sleep at night. Nobody could tell me that I wasn't going to achieve my goals or stop me from reaching my dream but me.

In addition to not letting yourself—or anyone else—be the reason you're not where you want to be, it is very important that the people you keep around you are positive. Having friendships with motivated people like yourself will encourage you to keep pushing forward to obtain your goals. If you are a person with goals in life, you shouldn't have friends who discourage you or who aren't motivated themselves to take advantage of opportunities that life presents them. Just remember: you are a reflection of the company you keep.

If you don't really have any friends, there are some benefits and some limitations to that choice. Pros include being able to get more things done without others holding you back; not having to deal with people who will encourage you to do something you don't feel is right; and learning responsibility for yourself. On the other hand, if choosing to remain distant, remember that you are in charge of keeping yourself motivated, holding yourself accountable if you are not where you want to be, and staying focused alone. Also that could put a hindrance on networking opportunities. Either choice you make with regard to the company you keep will benefit you if you make it benefit you.

Another part of being focused is by treating every day like it's your last. To be perfectly clear, tomorrow isn't necessarily promised to any of us, so it's important that you put as much effort as you possibly can into everything you do. Developing this type of mentality will help you handle any challenges that come your way. The reasoning behind this mentality is simple: not worrying about whether tomorrow is promised to you will automatically trigger your mind to reject fear and worry, allowing you to put all of your energy into anything that comes your way and keep the phrases "I can't" and "I quit" at the very back of your mind. The thought "I can't do this" should never cross your mind, because everything that has been done can be done better—you are that fresh, bright mind that can see things in ways that nobody has or may ever see. That's the big reason why companies bring in fresh minds to work for them—a person on the outside who hasn't been affected by the company has no reason to develop a biased opinion and therefore should have a "Why can't we do things this way?" mentality. Developing a habit of questioning things that don't sit right for you as well as improving conditions around you shows your optimism about everything you hear, see, and experience.

When getting focused, everyone has a particular way of doing things, but simply establishing yourself as an optimistic person early on will do wonders for you throughout your entire life.

B. PREPARING FOR THE STANDARDIZED COLLEGIATE EXAMS

The fact that you are now in the process of getting focused and making yourself more knowledgeable is a great start, but you still have a little ways to go. Unfortunately, filling out an application and submitting it to a college isn't that simple. Most colleges require you to take standardized admissions tests so that they can see if you have the proper analytical and writing skills that dictate whether you will be successful and a good fit for college. The higher your score on the college admissions test, the better your chances are of getting into a good college. Different colleges accept students based on various scores so it's helpful to have an idea of what scores the colleges you're interested in are accepting, and you can often find that by going to the college's website or by calling the college. Preparing for the college admissions standardized test may seem hard, but when taking the time to study and prepare yourself, it's not about how hard it is, it's about how you approach things.

First and foremost, take advantage of practices tests early on, because practicing will raise your comfort level when it comes time to taking the real tests. Don't wait until the last minute, because in doing so, you'll have already accepted defeat and basically said that there is no chance of passing. When preparing for the tests, the three R's—reading, writing, and arithmetic—are the focal points on each exam. Online sites for college admissions exams cater to specific subjects on the exam that you may need to pay more attention to in order to build your confidence. Finding a quiet place like a library or coffee shop to study in will help keep you focused as well as block any distractions or disruptions around you. A lot of times, libraries have study areas set aside for groups preparing for standardized tests. When it comes to preparing for the college admissions standardized test, I suggest not getting too wrapped up in the score you want to make; instead, focus on your weaknesses and then your strengths. This will help build your comfort level not just for taking the test, but also for what you may see on the test.

With everything wrapped up preparation-wise for the test, it is important to realize that if you are not satisfied with the score you make on the test, there should be no loss in hope. The reason we plan ahead is so that we always have time to make adjustments if things don't go the way we imagined. For those who are late in taking the exam, there are always other means to getting into college, such as attending a two-year college and transferring afterward to the college of your choice. For some, that is the easiest route because you won't be directly in your major of study—you can get your core classes out of the way and then transfer into your major at your college of choice. Also, for those who prefer to attend a two-year institution, you will most likely still have to take a college placement exam that will determine which core class level you will start off in. This exam is usually computer based and contains similar focal points to the standard college admissions exam.

Since the standardized tests are usually timed, you'll want to make sure that you don't spend a lot of time on one problem or in one particular section. In these situations, put a mark by the question or section and move forward; when you finish the remaining questions or section, come back to the ones you skipped. If you don't know the answer to a question, don't panic—instead, try the cancellation method.

To use the cancellation method, look at the problem's answer choices and single out each option that you know or feel doesn't make sense. The cancellation method is a better solution than just guessing at the answer, because you at least put some thought into answering the question. Never rush through a test, because you are liable to make more mistakes such as selecting the wrong answer, skipping a question or page, and even choosing two answers for one question. Once a section is complete, don't worry about the answers you marked, especially if you have more sections of the test to go. Doing so will only get you worried about not scoring highly enough in that particular section, which will then affect how you answer the questions in the next section.

When taking these standardized tests, the right mindset is that you are going to leave everything with the test. In other words, you're going to give it 110 percent and have no worries or regrets afterward. Once you get your scores back, it is important—and I stress this very much—that whatever your score is, whether it be above what you wanted, what you wanted, or even below, that you always remain optimistic and never take on a pessimistic attitude. When I say to be optimistic in your thinking, realize that a standardized test does not define you as an individual; you must keep moving forward to get into college. There are very smart and confident people who aren't great standardized test takers but are brilliant in the classroom, so never dismiss your goals and dreams because of one minor setback. Remember that no matter what your score, you have to move forward and not worry about how badly you did or how close you were—college is still on the table. By following this plan of preparing early for testing, you also allow yourself to retake the tests to aim at achieving a better score.

Depending on your score, certain colleges will either accept you or not accept you. Not getting accepted where you want does not mean that you won't be successful. People place a lot of stress on themselves to get into a great college, but the fact that they are entering college and taking steps to better their future is a wonderful dream to aspire to.

C. EXAMINING YOUR FINANCIAL SITUATION

When preparing to enter college, I advise taking note of your current financial situation. Sometimes, people who don't excel in school or score highly on their standardized collegiate admissions exam aren't fortunate enough to get into college. Also some people get jobs to save money before entering college which can be beneficial for your finances. However, financial aid and scholarships that are available should be a consideration when looking at your financial situation. Schools will have different tuition amounts, especially out-of-state colleges. The amount you'll pay in tuition depends largely on which school you prefer the most and where it is geographically.

When I say that college is an investment, I mean that many students will go into debt to make ends meet during their time at college. A lot of students take out loans for the entire duration of college to support themselves. Some students take out loans to build credit, and others do it simply because loans are easily accessible for college students. If you are the type of person who is scared of debt, which is a good thing, you have to realize that when it comes to loans, whoever is choosing to disburse that loan to you—whether it be your country, government, loan consultant, family, or friend—is investing in you to go through college, get your degree, and start your career.

The ability to use loans while in college has its benefits. Having a history of taking out a loan and paying it back is considered good standing for creditors and increases your credit score. A college loan would be considered good debt because it sets you up to receive long-term income. But we will touch more on that in a few chapters.

When looking at your finances, take into account that scholarships make a lot of things easier when you're in college. There are hundreds of national, international, state, and local scholarships and grants out there waiting to be claimed—you just have to look for them. Many scholarships and grants go unclaimed each year due to people not knowing about them or becoming discouraged about the qualifications needed to obtain those scholarships.

D. FINDING THE SCHOOL FOR YOU

Depending on what your particular field of interest may be, pursuing your education and going to college are very important.

To be honest, it is critical when you get to college that you take advantage of all the opportunities that are presented to you. A lot of people believe that if they can get into a big-name college that will be all they need to make it in their career. However, that is only partially true. Some companies as well as people have the power to open doors for you, and they often have a preference when it comes to selecting candidates from certain colleges. Some professional employers choose students from Ivy League schools; others focus on schools that have a high activity level with certain fraternities and sororities; and even others are just faithful to their alma mater. Don't let this dissuade you from going to college if you find out that you aren't accepted into your school of choice. It's important to realize that college is a fresh start for you in life, and it is equally important for you to know that college can be very competitive.

When you go to college, you have to stand out in your very own way to get noticed. Networking can help set up future opportunities. There are many different ways to stand out; you just have to find your niche and follow through with it. For instance, a person can stand out through good grades, volunteering, organizations, sports, and even just being a very vocal person around the college. There are many more paths to getting noticed, but these particular examples are some of the ways in which people put themselves in a position to get seen above everyone else.

A lot of times at two-year colleges, it's easy to stand out, but in some cases the opposite can happen when attending a four-year college. No matter what anyone says, there is nothing wrong with any college that has a high regard for strengthening the mindset of students. At many two-year colleges, the pace will be a little slower and will sort of mimic high school. A two-year college is a great option for anyone wanting to specialize quickly in a particular field that doesn't require a long duration of schooling. After high school, students have the option of taking their core classes at a two-year college and then transferring to a four-year university to start their major. This route often makes it easier to focus at a four-year college, because courses in this setting normally require more material review then at two-year colleges. Also make sure to check which class credits transfer over to the four-year colleges you have in mind, because not all colleges will accept the credits you get at the two-year college.

I certainly am not discrediting the curricula at two-year colleges, but it is a route that both high school students and people going back to school generally take, because they don't require as many qualifications to be accepted into. In fact, it is becoming more common that people start off at a two-year college rather than at a four-year college—students who go the two-year route will save more because two-year colleges often have a lower tuition cost.

If starting at a four-year college, it is a little easier to transition yourself as the years pass by, because you've been introduced to and become familiar with the college setting. With a four-year degree, there is more flexibility as well as opportunities to take with your education. Four-year colleges normally offer room and board, transportation, and other on campus activities to students. Those campus activities are what colleges use to attract a higher attendance.

Campus activities can include sports, social clubs, and campus events, and some campuses even have a reputation for being attached to certain popular figures in society. Tuition is much higher per year at four-year colleges than at two year colleges, because as mentioned before, they offer more amenities than your average two-year college. Another factor when considering the best school for you is housing & transportation. If you live on campus at the school of your choice, then you will likely pay to stay on campus, unless you're under a scholarship or special grant that may have special housing for you. For the people with or without cars, staying on campus is a great option because everything will likely be within walking distance. A lot of colleges are making it mandatory that students live on campus during their first semesters, which can be a great opportunity for some. When

I was in college, I chose to live at home and commute each day, because I found that I could get more things done and have fewer distractions in my way. I believe that it's a great experience to live on campus or away from home, but I had a personal agenda to carry out, so I did my own thing.

Lastly, I would say a college's reputation of the field of study you may want to be in should also be considered. It's best to feel comfortable knowing your school has a great prestige for producing graduates in whatever field you may be interested in.

STEP 2:

———

PREPARING FOR THE COLLEGIATE WORLD

When you finally decide on which college to attend, you have to be prepared for the world you're about to step into. A visit to the colleges or college your choice would be a great start to get a sense of where you will be. If you haven't already figured out what area of study you're interested in, that's okay—just realize that soon, you're going to have to make the choice.

Now don't make the mistake that I did when I went to my college orientation—being pushed into a major that you don't feel comfortable with. Because I was new, I just accepted it and tried to make the most of it. But later on, I realized that it wasn't for me, so I took back control of where I wanted to go in life by choosing the major that would help get me there.

When placed in a position like mine, you want to have at least thought about and researched your interests, but if you're not ready, simply tell them that you want to be undeclared at the moment. (My research came from taking online career assessment tests and reading about the different majors that each college offered.)

The next thing is to pay close attention to the orientation and presentation. You must remember that they are trying to sell their college to you, and at the end of the day, you are the customer who will make the choice and decide whether to spend the next few years of your life there. When touring a college, you shouldn't feel like you can't ask questions, because that's what the tour guides and collegiate staff are there for—to serve you. When we're young, we oftentimes get distracted when observing different scenes around us, so get used to carrying a small notepad with you to jot down what you want to know and expect to do.

The things to ask on a tour can encompass numerous topics, so plan ahead of time what you want to ask at the college. Helpful questions include how good the campus security is; what time the library is open and for how long; why the tour guide and any other staff members love the school; dorm rooms and their locations; and the whereabouts of certain locations and campus events, to name a few. This is also your chance to find out what majors the colleges are best known for and what the successful college hire percentage is in certain fields of study.

When I went on my tour, I asked to see the classrooms I would be studying my major in, I asked to meet the professors I would be learning from, and I even asked about some of the pros and cons of the college I was touring.

During the tour, take down as many notes as possible because when you get home, you will be comparing and contrasting against other schools, and you need to have as much information as possible to make your decisions. I took it a step further: I looked at each school's reputation in the news and accredited schools list and tried to recognize all the significant people in society who went there to see just how they benefited from an education at that school.

A. LEARNING YOUR NEW COLLEGE ENVIRONMENT

Once you have decided which college to attend, you need to learn where everything is, and that also goes for the people who just go to one class and then back home.

In order to be successful, it's important to know your surroundings so that you can take advantage of opportunities. You should start by getting a campus map and taking a tour of the different locations around campus. For those who feel like that could be a waste of time and wonder how that would help them upon entering college, the answer is simple: the chance of opportunities presenting themselves to you is pretty slim, so you have to actually go out and look for them. Just waiting on something to come will not always cut it.

When I say to look for opportunities, I mean do things like attending lectures, joining clubs, meeting new people at social events, and even shopping at that. It's important to position yourself around different personalities than your own, because that's part of how you will continue shaping yourself as a person.

When meeting new people, you have to pick and choose who you will socialize with. It may seem fun and adventurous at first, but it's important that you start your career off with people who are not only self-motivated but also have goals of their own to achieve. If you're a self-motivated person, that's great, but it never hurts to have friends who are motivated just like you. This isn't meant to discourage you from having fun, but remember that you're in college and that there's a reason why you're there. Attending lectures is a great, motivating way to stay focused, because colleges take time and resources to bring speakers to deliver a message to you.

For me, attending lectures in college was just another part that played a role in my success today. Listening to stories of how speakers carried themselves and steps they took to get to where they are inspired me to do whatever I had to do to put myself in a position to achieve everything I ever wanted. I was even more inspired after hearing about people who persevered through troubling and economic circumstances and ended up achieving their dreams and goals, especially when I knew that my circumstances weren't as hard as the circumstances that they had to go through.

Of course we always hear stories of people coming from poorer countries and not even knowing English, but somehow that didn't stop them from following their dreams, setting up their own businesses, and attending college. Often after lectures, the speakers will make themselves available to you one-on-one to answer any questions you have. That is your chance to get their perspective on certain issues or goals that you may want to know about.

From personal experience, I must tell you that depending on how constructive or even pessimistic advice from lecturers may sound, you should filter it—take the good for the good and the advice that doesn't help with a grain of salt. You should never let what other people say distract you from doing what you have to do to be successful.

Social clubs are another good thing to get into, and the clubs you decide to join can depend on whether you like being a part of large or small groups. Joining clubs in college is a good way to both get your foot in the door and build a rapport with people who are in your same position. It's beneficial to you because you're starting a track record of being a part of something outside of just going to class and studying all day. This is one thing that employers like to see, especially if you ever get the opportunity to play a major role in that social organization.

There are so many organizations out there that I can't talk about just one, but locating them is very easy. Your college's website is your resource for everything. Every organization held on the campus should have its name posted on the college website for you to explore. Also, the college website is another source for finding out what events are being held around campus and their locations. Some organizations have membership and material fees, so don't be surprised if they hand you an application with an upfront initiation fee. You should choose the organizations you want to be a part of like you choose your colleges—look at their activity on and outside of campus, their credibility and reputation around the college, and the people who are in the organization—because these will be your peers when you enter the club.

B. SCHEDULING CLASS FIASCO

Once you've learned more about your surroundings, now comes the tedious part—scheduling your classes for the semester. In college, you normally start off with what's called core classes. Your core classes consist of subjects like Math, Science, English, and History. Choosing which core classes to take first depends on how well you as a student can handle certain subjects at any given time.

A good idea to keep in mind when scheduling your classes is the times that the classes sit on. When choosing your classes, look at the ones that you feel may be a challenge for you at first and schedule them on days with less frequent classes. In other words, if you struggle in Math, then choosing to take a Math course on a two-day basis like Tuesday and Thursday or Monday and Wednesday will give you enough time to seek outside assistance from your professor or tutor throughout the week.

One popular way to schedule your classes is trying to aim at getting them all on Tuesday and Thursday (or just twice a week). This method is very effective in that you have more time and flexibility to study and relax, but it is your responsibility to take advantage of all the downtime you receive. A typical starting schedule for a college student is 12 hours of class, so you would no doubt have all your tests and quizzes on those two days. Whether you choose to attend classes every day or just once, twice, or three times a week, you must always make it mandatory that you keep up with the material.

Going back to college websites, class schedules can normally be found here for you to take a look at what's being offered that semester. Also, when choosing courses, you may hear not to take this professor or not to take that course because of how difficult or worthless it may be, but you have to realize that in college, you're going to take classes that you love as well as classes that you really don't care for. The method I liked to use when taking a difficult course was to tell myself that it was only temporary and that it wouldn't last forever. Some classes may require you to do a lot of studying or a lot of homework and may even have a lot of tests and quizzes which at times can be challenging. Just remember that this is all part of the life lesson of working hard for what you want which is a good grade, and sometimes taking the easy road can be good; but in the long run, learning to embrace challenges and even welcome obstacles will eventually create a more powerful you. Take my word for it—when you graduate, you will face challenges in life that are a lot tougher than that Physics or Engineering course.

When choosing classes, keep in mind that some courses are only offered once every two or three semesters or even just over the summer, and my advice to you is take them early—when it comes time to graduate, you don't want to hold up your graduation because of a class that hasn't come around yet. I have friends who were forced to put their graduation on hold because of that one class that they either kept putting off or could never get into because of how quickly it filled up.

A class schedule is your blueprint for each semester. When looking at blueprints, you study the quality and structure of what you're building. When architects and engineers want to design a building or product, they never wait until the day before the project is due to start designing their model; they look ahead to weigh their options and the positives and negatives of the moves they're trying to make. Don't wait until the last minute to figure out your schedule. Once you have your semester planned out, find your classroom locations ahead of time so that you won't be late on your first day.

When I was in college, I always ran across people who would show me their schedule and ask me to point them in the correct direction toward their next class. Being late your first day is bad form and very unprofessional. I realize that some circumstances may arise where you can't help being late to class, but you have to look at it like being late on your first day of work—it's just not professional or respectful to your professor and your classmates.

C. MAKING YOURSELF KNOWN TO THE PROFESSORS

The next step after getting your classes taken care of is getting to know your professors. A lot of students just go to class, wait until class ends, and leave. To plant the seed for success each semester, you want to make sure that your professors recognize you and know your name. Do not mistake this for being a teacher's pet—look at this instead as having an established network with the people who control whether you pass or fail the class.

In society today, almost everybody knows somebody with connections and power to make things easier for others, so why not have your professors as part of your collegiate network? Don't mistake your professor for your best friend because that is simply not the case, and it is important that when in the classroom, you show respect for what they're trying to teach. The effects of knowing your professors on a personal level can be very beneficial to your career. Professors are in a position to make some hard things very easy for you. When professors know who you are, you put yourself in a position to stand out, because they will have their eye on you and expect nothing but the best from you.

For example, say you are attending a concert and you see the performer standing 20 feet away from you. When that celebrity comes walking your way, I doubt you will turn around and run, but instead you will shout or stick out your arm to draw their attention. The only thing is, chances are slim that the celebrity will come to you, ask for your name, and remember you for the next six months, much less benefit your career. So why not introduce yourself to the professors who you will see more often and be in touch with who can help you later on whenever you may need help?

When you have to go to that job fair, which we will talk about later, getting a letter of recommendation from a professor with established tenure and respect around campus can work wonders for your career. This method works great when you have a great rapport with your professors. If they know you are always consistently working hard, on time, respectful, and dependable, then they will usually help you out in any way they can. However, most professors will be honest with you and tell you if you have disappointed them or showed no type of respect or consistency on tests, assignments, attendance, and even class participation. If you show interest in their material, then they will show a lot of interest in assisting you.

Many professors love engaging all of the students in the classroom when teaching new material. Remember, they're professors, so a lot of them take pride in doing what they love to do—teaching—and if you as a student show that you actually want to learn, then they will do anything they can to help you. If what I just said sounds cliché because you're supposed to participate in class, you'd be surprised to see how many classrooms are so quiet that you could hear a pen drop when the professor tries hard to encourage the class to participate. By asking the right questions and answering ones that the professor asks the class, you'll show that you want to be there and that you value the material being taught.

In college, some professors will quickly tell you that you don't have to come to class if you feel that you are wasting your time and theirs in the classroom. I've had a few professors who've displayed this type of attitude, but you shouldn't take those comments personally because they're just telling the truth. It's your responsibility to get to each class, study the material, do the assignments, and pass the tests and quizzes, not theirs. That's why first impressions are important not only in college, but in life too, because that's how you will be perceived by a lot of people whenever they see you or hear your name called. The first impression you make can also affect your chance of being involved with any outside networking opportunities that that professor may be involved with. Professors usually have outside connections to jobs that may interest you, and as long as you show them that you are responsible, respectful, motivated, and honest, there shouldn't be any reason why they wouldn't be willing to point you in certain directions for your career. When they refer you to someone, they are actually putting their credibility and reputation on the line from a reference standpoint.

D. HOLDING YOURSELF ACCOUNTABLE

Now that you are aware of the importance of establishing good communication with your professors, it is time to ensure that you hold yourself accountable for everything you take part in at college. This includes realizing that you are in a position to either help or hurt your career. I understand that you can't always plan out every single detail of how you are going to deal with certain things when you first enter college, but you can sure try. That's the purpose of a plan—if anything happens that causes you to steer away from that plan, you can always revert back to it and continue on your path.

Once you're on your own, you have to rely on yourself to make it through each and every day in college. There are no more parent-teacher conferences to put you in your place as well as no people to remind you to complete assignments on time. The only person you can count on to get things done is you. One of the best lessons I learned while in college was to rely on myself to get things done. It's like that in college, and it's also like that in the real world. Depending on your circumstances when entering into college, you may have to work harder than others, but that's a part of the journey we take to get to where we want to go.

In life, people take different paths and experience different things from each other, but at the end of the day, we all have to hold ourselves accountable when things don't go as planned. Do realize that nobody is perfect and there will be setbacks throughout college, but whatever happens, you have to keeping moving forward with your plan and goals. Life will not stop to wait on you—it keeps going, and the sooner you realize that, the more your mindset will continue to grow and become more open and aware to what's going on around you.

Learn to not blame other people if you make a mistake or don't get the results you want, because you alone will be the only person facing the results of your actions. While you're a student, take the time to educate yourself outside of the classroom as well. Become aware of what's going on around your city, state, country, and the world. Politics is one interesting topic to get into, because if it doesn't affect you now, it certainly will later on in life. You want to train your mind to have more of a social consciousness so you will be able to adapt and respond to anything that goes on around you. Having more of an in-depth social consciousness will allow you to examine things in a different perspective, and that's a priceless characteristic to have.

When you create a plan for how you're going to approach college, you must follow it all the way through. There are many people in the world today who have struggled to get to where they are and often end up falling short due to a lack of planning and just not knowing where they want to go in life. There is such a thing as students turning college into a career. That's correct—students actually spend years and money just attending courses and enjoying the college life.

I had a friend who was still a sophomore in his fifth year of college. When I became a senior, he became a junior, and I asked him why it took him so long to finish college when there was nothing standing in his way. He told me that he partied, didn't know what he wanted to do with his life, and took the laid-back approach so much that he fell behind in his classes, which caused him to have to retake courses over and over again. He then stated that the repetitive times of failing classes caused him to sit out an entire year of school. After asking him what changed his mind to turn everything around, he told me, "Jared, I came back with a plan, and I carried it out from start to finish."

The moral of that lesson is that the time spent away from college gave him a chance to reestablish himself, come back to school, and set himself up for future opportunities. A year later, I ran across him again, and I'm excited to say that he is now running his own business and appreciating the life-changing attitude that got him to where he is. However, even though it's great that he made it through his rough times, this isn't the path you need to go down—anyone reading this book can see that he wasted a lot of his time and his parents' time. That's why I continue to stress the fact that if you don't have any idea of how to get to where you're going, please start off by knowing where you want to go. Many of you know people in the exact same situation, and if you're one of them, it's best to just encourage them to continue trying to find their true calling for whatever they want to be in life.

If you are still having trouble focusing on how to establish yourself on campus and finding out what field you want to start in, each college has a student center where there are counselors available to discuss where you might be able to fit in. If you are still having trouble finding the right path, then you should probably think about taking a career service class, which is a course dedicated to helping students find out what they are good at in hopes of making a career out of it.

STEP 3:

MASTERING YOUR PLAYBOOK

It is now time to get in the game and follow through with everything you have prepared for. You have to go to work and put into action what you want to happen. Don't be discouraged or nervous at this point, because the challenge is here for you to carry out your plan. Just like in sports, when you want to win something, you will learn and master the playbook to put yourself at an advantage over your opponent.

It helps to write down what you plan to accomplish and keep it in a location where only you know its whereabouts. Some people prefer to let everyone know what they want to do, which is great, but it's best to get your goals down on paper so you don't forget a single thing. When it came to my playbook for college, I studied other students in different cultures and countries to see how they overcame obstacles and persevered through tough times in college. Doing so helped change my whole thought process about goals and made me look at them as journeys rather than just goals.

To further elaborate on my study of different cultures, I read articles, blogs, and forums about those people who were able to accomplish all that they did, even the younger kids who were in college. I noticed that a lot of them had one particular topic in common: time management. They knew what was at stake and took advantage of the time they had to learn their course material. What I loved the most about discovering their use of time management was that if the work didn't get done, it was on them to have the discipline to get it done.

A. TIME MANAGEMENT

Time management is a critical issue in both college and in the world outside of college. In both college and life outside of it, I've learned that it's always better to use time to your advantage because it goes by so quickly. One of the things that I noticed in college is that a lot of students, including me, would always say how glad we were that Friday came, and we wished that every week was fast. I later realized that when I looked at my college days as just wanting them to fly by fast, that was actually life itself flying by.

On the days that flew by so quickly, I could have looked into other endeavors or even put more study time into my courses to get those A's that ended up being B's. Since I realized that a little too late, I want to stress to you all to not waste any chance of reaching your full potential due to lack of time management.

There are a few ways to benefit from proper time management. One way is to limit the social media distractions around you. First things first: while it's fun to watch television, surf the internet, play the radio, and even socialize over the phone, you don't have to rely on these items like you rely on the air you breathe to live. As humans, we can be easily attracted to things like social media that tell us what to think and do, because they have already done the thinking for us. The media can literally shape the real world into any type of environment they want, because we only see what they give us. When the media show us what they want us to see, they are telling the viewers how to perceive what they are being shown and how they need to feel about what is shown. This is not to discourage anyone from listening to the media, but if we simply limit the amount of time we put into viewing and listening to the media, we can focus that energy on more ways to better ourselves as current and future professionals.

A second way to handle time management is to create a list of important things and non-important things. With this list, you're giving yourself a firm idea of what business needs to be taken care of first and what can wait. For the people who have a hard time figuring out what the important and not-so-important things are in life, look at it like this: anything to do with your grades or a career in your field of study is considered part of the important side of the list. If it's catching that movie on television or attending that party this week, it goes on the not-so-important part of the list. These are just a few examples—I realize that each person is different, so you have to sort your list according to what's important to you and what isn't.

A third way to handle time management is to arrive early to any classes, meetings, I mean everything. Have you ever heard of the saying, when you're on time you're late, and when you're early you're on time? It is very true. Start by setting your alarm 30 minutes to an hour ahead of time so you can avoid any delays or setbacks that may occur. When I had an interview, for example, I would show up 30 minutes to an hour early to both show my professionalism and to get a feel of my surroundings. I call it throwing them off their game, because a lot of interviewers don't expect you to arrive so early. If someone gives you a set time to meet, you should be at that location earlier so that you won't be the reason for holding him or her up or miss an opportunity that could be offered to you. Developing this habit of being early will take you far in life.

A fourth way to handle time management is by knowing the exact amount of time you plan to put into learning your course material. For every credit hour course I took in college, I would multiply that by two and study the course material for that many hours each week. With a two-hour course, you would study that material for four hours that week and so on. Another good habit to get into is reviewing the material that you learned right after you get out of class. If you have back-to-back classes, try to at least go over what you learned each day while the material is still fresh in your mind, so that you can develop a good understanding of the material. This will prepare you for future quizzes and tests.

Before we continue on to the next section, I want to mention that getting your rest is a big part of time management. Make sure you give your brain and body an adequate amount of rest each night to prepare for the next day. I can't tell you how many times in college that I went day after day with just one, two, three, or four hours' worth of sleep under my belt. Getting a small amount of sleep may allow you to get more things done, but it is very damaging to the body when it continuously crashes each night due to lack of rest. That's why I say please make sure you are mentally and physically prepared every day by incorporating a proper night's sleep into your daily plans.

B. TEST TAKING

The time of taking quizzes and tests will continue from high school to college, and if you aren't a good quiz or test taker, now is the time to reconstruct yourself to be a professional about it. Whether you play a sport, work, or even spend huge amounts of time participating in your favorite hobby, you can be a great quiz and test taker. When you put a lot of time into learning how to do something you like or love, you become good at it because of repetition. Well, I have news for you: the same thing goes for your studies.

If you put as much time into learning your studies as you do your hobbies, then passing quizzes and tests shouldn't be a problem. When students study for many hours for a test and still don't feel comfortable with the material, that's when the professor should be brought in to assist. This is one reason why I mentioned establishing a network with your professors—they are the ones who can reassure you that what they put on the quizzes and tests will actually be what you've studied. If the professors hold study sessions and you feel like you know the material, you should still go to make sure there are no surprises when the day of the quiz or test arrives. I can't tell you how many times that I went to a study session and the professor mentioned extra material that would be on the test or even gave bonus points to people who came to the session to learn. The actions you take in preparing for a quiz or test can really make a difference.

During any quiz or test, you should be aware of how much time you have so that you don't waste too much time on one particular problem. When taking an exam, try using some of the methods I mentioned in the SAT & ACT portion of the book to help you preserve time and get through each question without a lot of hesitation. After the test, no matter how good or bad you did or think you did, don't reflect on it for too long, because that will distract you from accomplishing other goals that you've set.

Remember, not everyone does as well on a test as they think they should, but there is always a chance to make up for that failed exam. If you're in a class where the material builds off of each section—math or chemistry, for example—realize that you need to master your weak points because not doing so will likely hurt you on the next test. That's why another good way to prepare for quizzes and tests is by making sure you do the homework assignments for the course.

C. HOMEWORK & CLASSROOM SEATING

A lot of college professors have courses with optional homework assignments, but I suggest doing the assignments and taking advantage of any extra work. If you ever have trouble with homework assignments, don't rush to the tutor first to seek help. The best source to go to is the professor, so he or she can show you the proper way of handling the problems in the assignment.

Tutors are also a great source for help when you're having a hard time grasping a concept, but it's smarter to go to the person who will actually be testing you on the material.

The homework assignments for your classes can also be used as proof of your understanding of the material. For example, if you ever make a mistake on a problem and your professor knows that you consistently get it right on the homework , then he or she will sometimes overlook the test problem or even give you partial credit because of your innocent mistake. This is not to say that every professor will do this, but it can be used to plead your case to obtain a better grade or bonus points. I also noticed that a lot of students become deterred from asking questions in class regarding homework problems, because they were afraid of what other students may think. Please realize that you are there for yourself and nobody else, and no question is an unintelligent one. Sometimes you have to tune out outside interference from the people who are inconsiderate to those trying to learn. By sitting in certain locations, you can put yourself at an advantage.

A lot of students in college attending the first day of class tend to head straight to the back of the classroom to sit down. However, I suggest sitting closer to the front or the middle section of the classroom. Any distractions normally take place in the back of the classroom, and you certainly don't want to be blamed for something you didn't do. Some students may do well sitting in the back of the classroom, which is fine, but if you don't happen to be doing as well as you would like, then your seating choice should be the first thing put into question. Also, your professor probably won't be too excited to speak over students who continuously distract the classroom. If you spot that type of disrespectful activity, migrate away from it, and if it becomes too much of a problem, then address the matter with the perpetrator after class; if it continues to persist, let the professor know.

Don't ever feel like you can't put something that's bothering you to a stop out of fear of what the people causing the distractions may think. It's like I say, you are there to learn for your benefit and not theirs—you have to pass the course to continue on to your next point, and they don't. With the homework and seating taken care of, it's now time for the end of week check-off.

D. END OF WEEK CHECK-OFF

The end of week check-off is what I like to look at as a weekly self-evaluation of how well I performed each week. I look at the mistakes and missed opportunities that I was placed in and work out a way to position myself to have a more productive focus on things in the coming week. The check-off can be used for both college and beyond, especially in everyday life. This method is supposed to teach self-improvement in all aspects of life. There is always something that needs work in our life, because we as humans are not born perfect and nor will we ever be.

When doing the end of week check-off, I like to ask myself questions like, Did I give 100 percent of myself every day this week? Did I do all the assignments due this week and next? Are there any quizzes or tests approaching that I need to pay special close attention too? Those are just a few examples of how I conducted my personal check-off.

When I did my end of week check-off, my mindset was to always stay a week ahead in all my classes—that way if something unexpected came up, I wouldn't be behind. If I had a paper due a month in advance, I would go ahead and start researching the topic to gather information and write it immediately to get it out of the way. Doing things with a sense of urgency allowed me to ask the professor to proofread my work before the due date so that I would get an early glimpse of what my grade would be if my paper were due that day. Doing an end of week check-off will also put your mind at ease over the weekend, which is when many students choose to relax and enjoy themselves. I start my end of week check-off on a Thursday night, because that leaves Friday to contact any professors—if I misunderstood any assignments that were given, I would have the chance to receive clarification about what needs to be turned in or completed. Once your end of week check-off is complete, you are free to do whatever you like, because you got the important things out of the way.

E. ENJOYING YOURSELF

Now I know you're probably thinking wow, he's really going to tell us how to enjoy ourselves? But that's far from what I'm doing in this particular topic. I am all for enjoying yourself in college, but you should be very careful with what activities you take part in as well as the areas and people you socialize with. The easiest thing for a lot of college students, especially young people, is to be easily persuaded by their peers. When making choices about what activities to take part in, I want to stress that you exercise good judgment and not get involved in anything you may know or feel isn't right. At any point in life, especially when you're in college, getting into trouble can wreak havoc on your career and automatically place you at a disadvantage when trying to start your career.

Many companies do background checks before hiring someone, and you don't want to find yourself explaining something you think may be innocent or not important to your employer. Not to sound like a parent, but I have a friend who got into trouble with law enforcement at a party and was taken into custody. He was charged with disorderly conduct, and that stayed on his record throughout his collegiate years. To make it even worse, his specific major required him to have an internship with a company outside of school in order to graduate, but he could never do the internship because of the failed background check. Today, he is still trying to get his record expunged. So if you take anything from what I just told you, please just realize that your actions do have repercussions.

When growing as a person, a great characteristic to start exercising is your own personal judgment. You often have to be hesitant and concerned about new faces you meet, because college can be like a city, where you see someone new every day. Some people have honest intentions and mean well, but others could only focus on themselves and care less about how things you're involved in together may affect you. Since each person differs in how they utilize their time, I can only suggest and hope that you learn when it's time to have fun and when it's time to be serious. In college, some students party all throughout the week, on the weekends, and whenever they want, so disciplining yourself early on is a great way to remind yourself of what's important and why you're there. When I was invited to parties in college, I only went to the ones that time permitted me to attend. Whenever I went to a party, there would usually be people drinking, and I would often be asked to join in. My reaction to them was always, "No, I'm fine," because of the simple fact that before I went to college, I wasn't drinking, so why should I start now? Many of my peers would continuously try to persuade me to drink by saying that drinking would make any problems I might be going through better. I responded by saying that when you sober up, your problems are still there left unsolved, so that's not a solution.

My advice to them was to approach problems head-on and overcome any obstacles that were in their way. Back then, I wasn't trying to sound like a counselor, but I considered myself a friend helping other friends in need. After a while, I quit attending parties, because they were a continuous cycle that I knew I didn't want to be a part of unless they benefited my future. Now in my story, you saw how I wasn't easily persuaded, because I had personal morals that I had established for myself and that I wasn't trying to break. I'm also not trying to downplay going to parties, because they can be a fun way to meet new people and make connections. In the end, though, it's often better to socialize and put yourself around responsible people who are motivated like yourself. I continue further on with how to approach unexpected situations that will inevitably occur.

F. HANDLING UNEXPECTED SITUATIONS

In college, almost all students will have to deal with unexpected situations that range from feeling homesick or overwhelmed, classes beginning, losing interest in your major, academic trouble, money, and the list goes on. The reason I call them "unexpected" situations is because these different categories are not foreseen when you enter college. For starters, feeling homesick can range from feeling sad to actually physically feeling nauseated. Being homesick can make people withdraw socially because of the emptiness they feel. However, the best way to get over feeling homesick is by accepting your new surroundings and adapting yourself to become more open to new things.

I had a few friends who got homesick in college, and they dealt with it in very creative ways. A few of them started to work out in the gym, and others took up music courses as new hobbies to get into. A few of them made frequent trips back home to fill the void of missing their families. If you are far away from home, I suggest sharing your feelings with other peers who can identify with what you're going through, because they can show you how they coped with the issue when they went through it. It's never really good to let your feelings of being homesick—or really any negative feelings—build up, because it can be very distracting when trying to get work done. If you feel you can't connect with anyone or haven't socially made friends yet, I encourage you to go to the student center, because they have events such as meet-and-greets and student fun nights where social interaction is automatic, so students will naturally approach you.

I didn't know anyone when I was in college, so I went to the student center—that's where a lot of my networking on a student level began, and I met a lot of great people. The connections I made helped me to make good choices about my classes as well. When choosing courses, many students try to take as many as they can, because they want to jump straight into their major. While it's great to be excited for your major classes, some classes require more attention than others, triggering a shift of focus that can cause you to either fall behind or struggle in your other courses. If you ever find yourself in this predicament, first look at the way you're handling your workload, and formulate a solution to fixing the problem. I suggest seeing if there are any distractions, and make a point to discuss the course work with your professor if you are struggling. If you have covered all your areas and exhausted all your options in trying to fix the problem and there is still no result, another solution could be to drop the course and take it again next semester or year.

One thing to note about dropping courses in college is that they are marked on your transcript and can affect your grade point average if dropped after the set date passes for dropping classes. However, dropping a course that you're struggling in earlier on can help save your grade point average from being negatively affected. In college, I had my own structured list to justify whether I needed to drop a course or not. Usually before the drop date, you'll take a test that shows you how well you're doing so far in the class; how I did on the test and the classwork would justify whether I would drop the class or not. To me, it didn't make sense to start the semester off fighting your way back to the top when you have the opportunity to start at the top.

Everyone takes tests that they know they didn't do their best on, so how hard you commit to overcoming that minor setback is on you. It's really not good to get into the habit of continually dropping courses, so you should only do it if you feel that the course is overwhelming you at that point. There are often penalties for dropping too many classes, which can lead to a negative impact on your transcript. Colleges may have different policies when it comes to handling withdrawals. Typically, the letter "W," meaning "withdrawal," will appear on your transcript if you drop a class; a "WF," meaning "withdrawal failure," will appear if you drop a class after the drop deadline and will affect your GPA. This is something you may want to look into if you feel you may be dropping more than two classes. Another easy way to figure out whether you should drop is simply by talking to the professor, because he or she will be honest when letting you know whether you have a shot at passing or making the grade that you want in their course. This is another reason why it's always good to plan ahead and have a balanced course load that you know that you will be able to handle.

Some students take the maximum amount of courses that are allowed in a semester, but usually they will have to be approved to do so by their colleges. For example, at my college, the maximum number of course hours you could take was 21 hours. When broken down, those 21 hours are the equivalent of seven three-hour courses—that many hours can be a lot on a student. The maximum number of hours I have ever taken in college was 18, and that was hard on me because I was also the president of an organization at the time. If you ever feel overwhelmed, don't just sit there and struggle to even pass when the simple task is to just discuss your options for the course with your professor or counselor so they can help you.

A lot of times, too much work can deter people from following through with their major—and depending on how late it is in your college years, it can be another setback. I remember in my second year in college, I was finishing up my core classes and just starting my major courses. The more I got into taking courses in my major, the worse I felt, because I realized that I lost interest in the material. The excitement that I felt before I jumped into it was simply lost, and my motivation to continue through it began draining away.

For me, I would say that that was one of the scariest moments I went through in college—ever since high school, I had my heart set on being one thing, and when I finally got into it, I found out that it wasn't what I thought it would be. I consequently loss focus in everything else that I was doing; I started questioning what I was really in college for and whether college was even worth my time. During those trying times, I continued listening to lecturers speak and talking with established businessmen and women about their struggles, and that encouraged me to become more focused and driven to find my true passion.

I was able to discover what I wanted to do by joining a career services course, which then led me to finding what I truly wanted to do and make a career of it. By reverting to what I had previously advised and sticking with my own tailored playbook, I was able to regain my focus and continue forward with setting up my career. From that experience, I learned that the setbacks that we have are only long and hard if we allow them to be. It's best to try to not let any setbacks affect your grades in college, though because in the business world, some employers separate their applicants by GPA.

The GPA is a calculation of grade points divided by total hours taken. For example, if you take one three-hour course and two four-hour courses, and you get an A in the first course but two B's in the last two, your GPA would be a 3.27. The point values in college are as follows: A=4, B=3, C=2, D=1, F=0. The above example can be written out as, 4*3=12, 3*4=12, 3*4=12, then added up to be 36. Then divide 36 by the total number of course hours—11—and the GPA will be 3.27. Don't worry if this seems a little confusing; there are numerous GPA calculators online that will help you figure out where you stand with your score. Also, many colleges have a built-in GPA to allow you to calculate your GPA to their standards.

You should be very careful with the classes you take, because whether you pass or fail and depending on if you choose to drop a course (before or after the drop deadline), your GPA will be affected and could potentially cause academic trouble. A lot of students don't realize that once your GPA starts dropping, the harder it is to pick it back up. When your GPA begins to fall, your college will be the first to let you know—they will penalize students whose GPA falls below the school-suggested GPA limit. If your GPA drops below the limit, most colleges will respond by issuing an academic warning; if matters get worse, probation; and if that gets worse, suspension could be next. Each college decides how to handle students with academic trouble.

Colleges do give students a chance to fix their grades, so while getting something like an academic warning isn't really something to smile about, it's not the end. However, these types of warnings and suspensions will appear on your transcript, which can stand out significantly. A lot of employers ask to see transcripts to determine how well you did in college, and that could be the last thing you want them to see. If you get into the dilemma of being placed on academic probation or suspended, then you must realize something: it's not how you got yourself in that predicament—it's how you respond and correct yourself to fix the issue.

One of my friends got put on academic probation and was afraid that the university would kick him out of school and his parents would thus find out. I suggested looking at what went wrong and what caused him to be placed on probation so that he could overcome the obstacle. After a semester passed, he told me that he focused more on learning and limited his social life to just a few times a month instead of every day. This caused a significant turnaround for him—he was taken off academic probation and avoided suspension. In fact, he now works for a marketing firm and is doing quite well for himself.

Even though an academic penalty will be put on your transcript, don't let that deter you from continuing to work hard—remember, it's only disturbing if you allow it to be. I especially want freshmen to pay close attention to this, because it affects you the most. When you first enter college, your GPA hasn't been established yet, so it starts off at zero—your high school GPA doesn't transfer to college, so you're basically starting fresh. It's good to start off by taking courses that will build and strengthen your GPA. Ending your first semester with all A's would make your GPA a 4.0, which would be great. However, if you don't do so well your first semester, then your GPA will start off low and you'll end up fighting to get it back to where it needs to be to avoid any academic penalties. The best course of action is to start out strong and set a goal for obtaining a high GPA. If you have the chance to take summer courses before your actual fall or spring semester begins, you can build your GPA by just focusing on one or two courses.

Another unexpected issue in college that eventually comes around is money. In college, you'll realize that it is hard to have fun without money, because that is a major factor in being on your own. Everyone in college has a different circumstance, ranging from being fortunate—where money isn't necessarily a problem—all the way to not being so fortunate, where a lack of money can halt a lot of things. Having no money can certainly be a discouraging experience to go through, but there are ways to overcome this.

For starters, many students take out loans to help them cover school materials like books, which can be expensive, and fees for room and board. A lot of times, students who aren't used to handling large amounts of money will spend their loan to enjoy themselves instead of saving the money. To avoid having to pinch pennies when you get into college, I suggest setting up multiple bank accounts to avoid sticky situations and to help overcome any emergencies that may arise. I would suggest a checking and savings account. Being young and having access to a significant amount of money will entice you to start spending on yourself, and you could end up throwing all your money away. If you start your own bank account and let your money build interest, then later on you will have made a little extra cash for having money just sit in your account. If you go the loan-free route like I did and just use grants to pay for everything, then that's still great—whatever money is left over should still be put in the bank. Since tuition continues to rise each year, you should always create a safety net to have some room for a few financial moves if needed. Those are just a few ways to avoid some unexpected situations; I will talk more about handling and earning money later on.

STEP 4:

———

TIME TO EARN AND LEARN

I encourage everyone in college to learn the value of a dollar early on. Having a job teaches responsibility and accountability as well as helps with your time management. Before you get a job, though, make sure you have all of your priorities in order. There is a difference from wanting a job and needing a job. I believe both ideas are great—wanting to make your own money early on is a very intelligent move. When you're in college, making your own money sounds good, but you must not forget why you are there in the first place. I say this because if you get a job and make a significant amount of money and go to college, getting used to making that money could possibly deter you from your studies. I've had numerous friends drop out of school because they got jobs making 12 dollars an hour at some factory, which at the time sounded good, but it's not a long-term solution. If you get a job, you should treat it like another class and be attentive, respectful and on time.

For the people who have to have jobs and go to class at the same time, time management and organization are crucial. It is not uncommon for people to balance work and school at the same time, so it can definitely be done. It takes a lot of discipline to understand that you have to balance studying, attending classes, and getting much-needed rest. However, it can be done. Plenty of my friends have done work-study programs in order to earn money for tuition and whatever else they needed for school. Work-study is a great route to take, because the college will look at your class schedule and actually prepare a work schedule around that based on how many work-study hours you are allowed to take.

While working in college, if you are able to gain employment with a company that offers certain benefits like insurance and 401k plans, it's great to start early. If you want to make money and are having trouble deciding on what jobs to take part in, you shouldn't be afraid to try something new. I encourage pursuing any job that is different from what you may be used to—you want to gain experience, and you don't want to limit yourself to just one area. When I was in college, I had my own personal computer consulting firm where I would charge people to assist them with their computers; I worked at the botanical gardens and even wrote opinionated articles to gain a few extra dollars, so don't limit yourself to what you think you can do. There are a lot of ways to make money in college; the only thing you have to do is find out which way is best for you.

To break it down even further, it's important to realize that everything around you is an opportunity waiting to be taken advantage of—you just have to find it and make it work for you. The entrepreneurial route should not be overlooked. Once you figure out what you want to do, establish a simple business plan that includes both startup costs and what it will cost to maintain the business. The next step is taking that idea or potential venture and figuring out whether you have competition; if so, what's your competitive advantage over your competition? Make sure that you will have patience with whatever you decide you want to do, because even though some businesses take off quickly at the beginning, others may take a while before pulling in any type of substantial revenue. Whatever you do, never be afraid to try and never let your fear control you, because that can spread and weaken you in other areas of your life.

A. WORKING, INTERNSHIPS, & NETWORKING

Another great way to earn money and experience in college is through internships. An internship is basically on-the-job training that people go through to gain experience in their field of interest. There are two types of internships: paid and unpaid. You are looking to gain experience from a business standpoint, so I'm not going to say that paid internships are better—the incentive is money, but learning how the internship will benefit you is what's important. I've had the opportunity to take an internship out-of-state to gain experience, meet new people, and actually learn how to conduct myself in a corporate setting outside of campus.

I looked at my internship as more of a personal skill-building experience—I no longer feared making mistakes when I started my first real career-related job after college. That internship taught me about politics in the corporate world, project management, working more efficiently on a team, and not being afraid to voice my opinion when I felt something was either wrong or needed attention. For those of you who don't really want to travel, there are usually internships available on campus for you to partake in. To find internships, you can either search online for different companies through their websites, or the college website should also have a listing of internships on campus.

Another great thing about jobs and especially internships is that they allow you to create strong networks. When working, it's important to introduce yourself to your co-workers and other employees. Don't assume that people will always come up to you and introduce themselves, so start making that a habit. I remember when I was interning at one company as a technology administrator, and the only people I knew within the whole company were the eight people who worked in my area. It wasn't until I decided to come out of my shell of being a student intern that I started to meet new people, and pretty soon people were telling me about new positions that were coming up soon, taking me to lunch, and even offering me valuable college and life advice. It's always great to work with people who have been down the road you're on, because they have valuable knowledge to pass on to you.

When you meet these people, make sure to remember their names. It's important to realize that anybody new you meet is a person, and if they've taken the time to remember your name, then you should definitely do the same. Having and showing respect towards others can and will carry you a long way in life. It's also important to take advantage of the opportunities that an internship can give you. Regardless of whether your internship is boring or exciting, you have to work smart and hard; if you do those two things, you will definitely stand out.

At my internship, I was known for doing everything with a sense of urgency—I was even given the title of "Speedy" because of my fast responses and ability to do both the easy and hard work quickly. I was told that I made other employees look bad and that I needed to slow down, but in actuality, I felt that since the company took the time to interview me and choose me to come aboard, I didn't want to disappoint. When you're giving your job your all, you don't worry about anyone else except for you and the tasks at hand. With this mentality, I ended up meeting and networking with the CEO of the company I was interning for, and he told me to keep pushing forward—that's exactly what I continued to do for my entire duration there. Once you're through with your internship, it's wise to get into the habit of sending thank you letters. This reminds the employers of who you are and how thankful you are for the opportunity that they have given you. If you are fortunate enough to have a paid internship, then this is a great start to saving money and building a good reputation.

B. BANKING & CREDIT CARDS

When I was in college, the two words that I heard most often alongside my regular education was banking and credit. The banking part was easy for me, because all I had to do was create an account, put my money into it, and let it sit there and build whatever interest that it could build. The credit part was a little more difficult for me to swallow—I was so fearful of being in debt that I just created a habit of paying for everything in cash. However, even though the way I did things was very beneficial to me because I didn't have anything attached to my credit history, when I graduated, it was hard for me to get any good deals or awards because I had no credit history.

My advice to you in regards to dealing with credit is to establish a credit history early on, because it takes time to build a good credit score. If you decide to begin building your credit score early, I highly advise not going over your limit. For example, I had a $300 limit on my first credit card, so I made small purchases and paid off the credit card each month. My goal was to establish a rapport with the credit card companies and show that I was trustworthy and dependable early on. Due to my consistency with my credit card, my limit began to increase more and more, but I still disciplined myself and paid off the credit card at the end of each month.

Another good source for building credit is through loans. Student loans are usually attached to your credit history, and when you graduate, you will be responsible for making the loan payments in a timely fashion. A lot of people told me to keep deferring my student loans until I was ready to start paying them back, but when I graduated college and was fortunate enough to start my career, I just went ahead and started making monthly payments.

When dealing with school loans, sit down with your loan counselor and consider all your options together. During your session with the loan counselor, remember to ask the entire how, when, where, and what if questions, because they can tell you how it will affect you going forward. I highly recommend starting early when managing your funds. It's a sad thing when you get older and end up starting at the bottom with your credit and lack of funds because of the lack of discipline you chose to show with your finances. Also, start reading more books on investing, saving, 401k plans, and learning where your money comes from and how it grows. I guarantee that once you start studying your own finances alongside your schooling material, you will not only have a strong outlook for your career but for your personal finances as well.

In actuality, your finances and your career can sort of be neck and neck with each other. When I say this, I mean that you will make a certain amount of money with your career, which is considered your income. If you are growing with your career, your finances should be shaping up at the same time as well. It's never good to be living paycheck to paycheck, because that shows in some form or fashion that your ability to manage your funds is not up to par. For example, when I was in college, I worked and did internships for the school to gain experience and money at the same time. I managed to save up $8,000 at the age of 21 from being in college and working. When I had that money, I started looking for ways to become more business-minded to increase my financial earnings—I started researching the stock market and how it worked, looking at IRA's to put my money in, and even investing in small start-ups to create another bridge for having more money come to me.

While it's great to save, it will take you a lot longer to accumulate additional income if you're just taking every paycheck and putting it into the bank. While you're young, now is the chance to take more risks because you have no intentions at the moment of planning for retirement. If one thing doesn't work out, then try something else—you have to find your niche. College was a great place for me to start, because I would get free advice from my economics professors—they were available to me and couldn't charge me personally. By making sure that you're managing your money well and establishing good credit, you will definitely be moving in the right direction.

Since you're either in or preparing for college now, do realize that both the accumulation and building of credit will take time, so patience is a great virtue to have. Speaking from personal experience, it was hard to do anything in this position without money and especially credit. In today's world, credit is basically considered more trustworthy then your actual vocal word of, "I manage my finances successfully" and "I promise to pay you back." When I entered the corporate world, I found that it was very difficult to purchase a nice car or home as well as rent an apartment because of how low my credit score was. However, some companies will take you being new into consideration and still take a chance on you.

To simply build my credit, I knew that the easiest thing to do was to get a credit card. Although getting a credit card may sound easy, I didn't get one until after college, and very few credit card companies would even take a chance on me. After continuous effort in trying to find a company that would take a chance on me, I got my first credit card with a limit of $300. With that amount, I would charge $150 to my card each month and pay the whole thing off by the end of the month to establish a good rapport with the credit card company. Once I consistently kept this task up, my limit soon increased to $500, and I then started increasing my purchases and so on. By doing this, I was building my credit score to a stronger figure. Don't get too tied up into your credit score, though, because it takes time to build, and it will definitely take more than a year at that.

Another way I built credit was by taking out a secured loan against my savings account. By doing this, I allowed the bank to put a hold on a certain amount of money in my account, and I just paid them monthly payments on what they were holding. You're basically taking a loan out, but you're using your own money as collateral, and that reassures the bank that they won't lose anything—as long as you continue your payments, it will go down as a plus for your credit report.

C. MAKING SMART FINANCIAL CHOICES

I know that I've touched on ways to conduct yourself on a collegiate level, but now I feel the need to speak on practicing financial self-control. When I was in college, I received reimbursement funds and worked at the same time. At first, I wasn't always financially self-disciplined because I really love nice things. I would use my paycheck to splurge on the latest and greatest products. The things I bought ranged from clothes and fine dining all the way to electronics. I spent my checks as soon as I received them.

The thing that got me to change my ways with spending my entire paychecks was never having any money left over in case I had issues with my car repairs, school material, gas, and food—I knew that I had to create some boundaries for myself to break out of that habit. A large number of college students can probably agree with me on this one, because when students get their reimbursement checks, the malls and shopping stores begin to flood with college shoppers anxious to spend money. The way I broke out of the habit was by buying things for college that were low in cost that I would use for the entire semester. For example, when it came to fashion, I didn't always need the high-priced name-brand items, so I settled for a lot of mediocre design wear. To be quite honest, a lot of the non-name-brand items out there still look better than some of the name-brands, but that's just my personal opinion.

Next, I set budgets to control my spending throughout the week. I calculated how much gas it took to get me from point A to point B, how much food cost per week, and how much money I wanted to spend when hanging out with friends. The great thing about this method was that any uncontrolled spending that may have occurred that week was my own fault, because I had a budget and chose not to follow it; if I went over budget one week, I would then subtract that out of the next week's budget. If I needed a computer, I considered that a great investment, so I looked for a decent one with a great warranty but a low cost. A lot of times, there are computer shops around the area that cater to student deals on computer repairs as well as warranties on their own products for students to buy. I favored buying long-term items that would be of more constructive use to my career rather than items used solely for my enjoyment.

For example, video games: I love video games, but instead of buying them, I would simply rent them or find a friend to let me borrow one instead of spending money on something that was just going to sit on my shelf collecting dust. I purchased books that were constructive, software that I could use for business ideas; if I wanted to learn a new language, I would buy the books or software to help me study.

Another thing that I did was decrease the amount of time I spent at social settings like parties and festivities that cost money to get into, instead settling for any free activities that took place. My college friends called me cheap and stubborn, but when it came down to going out, I always had money and they didn't because of their uncontrolled spending. I practiced this method for two years straight, and it felt great having funds to access whenever I wanted. I fell more in love with knowing that I was no longer in a situation where money could all of a sudden become scarce to me. The availability of funds only increased my confidence more—not because it was materialistic, because that's a false sense of confidence, but it gave me reassurance that I would be financially okay in college as long as I continued this method.

STEP 5:

THE END OF THE SEMESTER

The end of the semester is finally here, and now is a time to congratulate yourself on making it through. Finally, you have taken your last set of exams, and you can relax a bit before your next semester. However, keep in mind that while the semester may be over, there are always things you can be doing while you have downtime. I always replayed each semester of college back in my mind to examine how well I performed during that time. I looked for mistakes that could have been avoided, so I would know how not to make them in the next semester. Some mistakes I would look for were not participating as much as I should have, not attending enough study sessions, things that became distractions, having a lack of time management, and having a lack of organization.

In college, sometimes things beyond your control are subject to happen. If you end up in a situation that you don't know how to come out of and you see it's affecting your classes, you have to overcome it. I suggest examining the problem—figure out if the problem can be solved and try to fix it. Also, know your personal limitations; if you are still struggling, seek advice from a counselor. Whatever the problem may be, remember that as long as you believe in yourself and trust that you will get through the issue, then you will be able to overcome anything.

For example, when I got into a car accident that completely destroyed my car, I was more thankful that I had made it out alive than having a car. After a few weeks had passed, I struggled with trying to find ways to class. I also learned that I was being sued, I didn't have enough money to cover all of my books, and my grades began to drop because of everything that I was going through. However, I had a lot of faith that I would overcome the situation, and I handled each problem as it came. Whether the problem was of high importance or low importance, I always looked at it as a whole and figured out ways to chip away at it until it became a small problem and eventually went away. That's how I handled problems in college, and that's how I continue to handle problems today.

When your semester in college ends, if you know for a fact that you could have approached things better, then just accept the fact that you didn't follow through with what you wanted to do. Once you've accepted that you could have done better, you can start looking at what it will take to avoid making the same mistake twice. The worst feeling to have is after final exams when you're hoping that you either got the grade you want or that you even passed the course.

When I first entered college, I remember the nervous feeling like it was yesterday when it came to end-of-year final grade postings. I had nowhere near the knowledge that I have now, but all I can say is that due to lack of preparation, I didn't always get the results I wanted. To relieve myself from ever having to go through that again, I started reassessing the way I carried myself and how I approached tasks at the end of every semester. The saying "practice makes perfect" is very true because I became my own worst critic, which can sometimes be a good thing and sometimes a bad thing. After each semester, I gave myself my own reality check to make sure I stayed in line with my priorities and goals.

A. REALITY CHECK

It's important to remind yourself of why you are where you are and why you are doing the things you are doing, especially in college. I know what it feels like to have a great semester as well as what it's like to have a not-so-great semester. When I had my great semesters, I felt like I was on top of the world and wanted to stay there; but when I had my bad semesters, I felt ashamed and even questioned the reason I was in college.

Every human being is different, and while some people may be able to handle not achieving their goals pretty well, it is very difficult for those who can't handle it. My feelings of self-doubt would occur only when I had bad semesters. I expected things to not always be so difficult and I had preconceived notions on what it would take to accomplish this and that, but I would always forget how important it was to approach everything with a sense of urgency, focus, and seriousness.

When I had good semesters, I noticed that I procrastinated when it came to the next semester—the problem was that I never had a consistent flow in the way I approached things due to my assuming that the next semester would be like the one before. Once I broke myself out of that habit, I realized how important it was to remain motivated to continue forward in each semester. In college, when everyone is through with classes and finals are out the way, a lot of students have a hard time continuing forward and quickly getting back into their same groove.

The advice I want to share that I used whenever I came from a long or short break is to keep motivated by staying in contact with other people who were motivated; consistently reading articles about how well my major would be in the economy; working out and eating better; reading self-help material; and watching motivational videos. At the end of each semester, I made sure that I always kept in touch with friends who were motivated just like I was. Having friends who were excited about accomplishing goals as well as friends who were competitive made it a lot of fun for me to want to keep up. I liked that whenever I read about my major, I would always hear how well it was doing in the economy and around the world. I highly encourage every student to keep tabs on the progress of how their major is playing out around the world. Whether you want to be a doctor, lawyer, engineer, actor/actress, nurse, scientist, or whatever your interest is in, there is always information available on how your major is doing in the business world.

There are always articles that may discourage people from following careers in certain majors, but if you feel strongly about something, then you should follow through with it. I have friends who took up acting, for example, and while they graduated with a performing arts degree, they are still waiting for their big break—but it was something they felt strongly about in college, so they followed through with it and have chosen to continue forward. While I used acting as an example, almost every major is very competitive because you must remember that there is always somebody in the world with the same dream as you—who wants it more, who is willing to work hard for it, and how you all approach obtaining that goal will be the determining factor when it comes to success. I've always held the notion that while you're sleeping at night, there is somebody around the world working hard and training to take your spot, so you have to always want to put yourself in a position to better yourself each day.

Another way I stayed motivated is by exercising during periods of downtime. Exercise has been known as a good tool for increasing brain function, getting the body feeling more energetic, and lowering the high levels of stress that may pile up on you. When I finished a semester that I knew I didn't do my best in, I would often have high levels of stress around that time. I was able to relieve that stress through exercise. When I worked out, I was able to put my stress behind me, and that exercise allowed me to present a new outlook when faced with challenges.

Everyone deals with stress in their own ways, but I recommend physical fitness because it helps the body and mind to relax, and plus it allows you to get into shape. I also suggest eating healthier. Heavy foods can make you feel sluggish and actually slow you down when trying to focus. I incorporated more fruits and vegetables to give me the proper nutrients that I needed to stay feeling better and more energetic.

I strongly believe that to gain inspiration, it helps to read inspiring stories of others and how far they went to accomplish their goals. Looking at all the obstacles and poor circumstances a person has gone through and the things done to overcome them can be very inspiring to conquer any problems that you might have in your way. I don't think that people should just stick to inspiring stories, but I encourage you to read more to get a chance to go inside the authors' worlds that they are presenting to you—read their insights or stories and open your mind to the whole new world they've created for you. When anyone asks me for advice on how to start loving to read or even making reading a daily task, I tell them to look at all books as new worlds. In each and every book you pick up and read, there is something you can learn and take away. Reading helps open your mind to new things and enables you to improve your overall focus as well as your vocabulary.

When I was trying to improve my small vocabulary in college, instead of just reading the dictionary all day, I would simply read books on different topics and look at how the authors used words to describe what they were talking about. A lot of young people may think that reading is a waste of time and they could be doing something better like playing with electronics or sleeping, but I promise you, reading is a great way to boost imagination and even inspire you to look at your surroundings with a different perspective.

Alongside reading, motivational videos are another good source I would take advantage of when I needed some type of inspiration to stay motivated. This can range from music to watching speakers do seminars—they're not just for the older generation, but the younger generations as well. The same concept is to better yourself and help you to reach your full potential. I would watch motivational videos while constructing my resume and listen to keywords to help my resume stand out.

B. RÉSUMÉ

For those of you who have never made a résumé before, it's basically how you sell yourself to a potential employer. When you go shopping at the mall, you look for sales and good deals that catch your eye, and a lot of times a clerk will approach you and try to promote the product so that you buy it. One way to look at your résumé is that you are the product and the employers are the customers. If you want to sell a product to a customer, you have to present it in a way that will grab the customers' attention and allow them to become interested.

Since you are the product, your résumé is a representation of yourself on paper. To put it even simpler, the more you put on your résumé, the more you will stand out. When creating your résumé, look at different styles to try and separate yours from everyone else's. Many people fail to realize that using keywords inside your résumé can actually help it become more eye-catching. When companies scan through different résumés, they look at the classes you've taken, your job history, awards and achievements, special skills, volunteer work, GPA, and references.

Focusing on keywords is important because a lot of companies have computers that scan through the résumés that are submitted online and randomly pull out the ones that meet particular criteria. The best way to get creative is with your résumé. For example, let's say I worked at a computer shop fixing computers. I wouldn't just put "computer repair person" on my résumé; instead, I would put that I was a computer support technician at computer shop XYZ. If you worked at a coffee shop and your only job was setting up the display, serving coffee, and checking out customers, you would write you were a customer sales associate at restaurant XYZ.

The main point is to understand that you have to be creative with your titles, because anybody can call themselves a clerk or PC tech. If you're ever talking about specific job skills that you've acquired, it helps to use bullet points. I highly advise not trying to describe your job functions and skills in long paragraphs—you want your potential employer to be able to easily spot a specific point that they may be interested in, and bullet points look more professional and are better for document organization. It can also be a little difficult to figure out whether or not to list all your jobs on your résumé, but I suggest including any job positions that may have recognized you for your leadership, being great with customers, or anything else that would show the employer your different professional and personal qualities.

For example, I put a short "about me" section on the bottom of my résumé to grab the employer's attention. I used the section as a way to personally communicate to the employer since I wasn't there at the time. When I went to interviews, I would often be commended on my about me section—employers have admitted that when they see a particularly good résumé, one of the first things that comes to mind is, "I wonder how that person is in person," so I figured I would make it easier on them and just give a heads up on what was to be expected.

Another thing to watch out for inside your résumé is the use of slang. Using acronyms like lol, tbd, and any type of informal language that you normally use with close friends and relatives can hurt you because it shows a lack of professionalism when it comes to your ability to produce formal documentation. A good thing to start doing is to learn how to have many different types of résumés for different jobs—prepare your résumé for that particular job, and don't have just one résumé that remains the same for every employer that may come into contact with it.

For example, if your major is culinary arts and you're interested in two jobs—one at a school and the second at one of the finest restaurants in America—you would want two different résumés that are specifically tailored for those jobs. With schools, you might talk about your background in learning nutrition for kids and daily meal planning; but with the prestigious restaurant, you would talk about your ability to multitask in a fast-paced environment and your special skills with customer service.

When preparing your résumé, one of the worst things you can do is try to match yourself to another person—you are your own person and you have your own style that is different from everyone else, so never feel inferior if you see that another person has more experience or awards then you. That's why you work hard in college: to have something to show for all the days, months, and years that you put into pursuing your major of study. With résumés, it's always great to show some type of involvement with the community, college, organization, or some type of affiliation—it shows that you are committed to other things besides your work. Remember that when companies are making a choice on you, they know that they are not just getting the person you present on your résumé but all of you.

When I was in college, I strived to put something under each category to help me stand out from everyone else. My degree was in technology, so it was very competitive, especially at a college that hadn't yet made it into the collegiate technical arena against other schools. I literally had friends with whom I had shared the same major, who would try to copy my résumé to gain an edge on me. Some people would view that kind of plagiarism as unprofessional and just down right wrong, but I took it as a compliment— you always know you're going in the right direction when people want to focus heavily on what you're doing. When creating your résumé, there is a big difference between being creative with the way you word and phrase sentences and lying. If you get to a point to where you are putting down things you have no experience in, then you're basically lying to the employer's face.

If you're brought in for an interview and the employer finds out you falsified certain information, that interview can be a whole momentum shift when it comes to you being potentially hired. If an employer sees that you lied about something simple on your résumé, then why should they take your word for anything else on your résumé? If you have limited experiences and skills to put on your résumé, I suggest immediately doing both collegiate and personal projects to gain more knowledge in a short time frame. There are always ways for you to get better each day, and I took advantage of that significantly when I was in college.

Not only did I list my job experience and collegiate work on my résumé, but I also purposely created personal projects that I added to my resume. This showed the employer that I was persistent and content with studying my craft both inside and outside of class. If you're new to writing résumés, I suggest researching the different styles out there and personalize some to your liking. There are literally hundreds of books and articles online to help you choose a good fit. The student center is also a good source for helping students with their résumés.

You should have a cover letter to accompany your résumé for the employer to read. A cover letter allows you to briefly introduce yourself to whomever will receive your documents, which could be your interviewer. In the cover letter, you will explain to the reader who you are and why you think you are a good candidate for that position; make sure you tailor your experiences and skills to the job description. When applying for jobs, you want the employer to remember you, so a résumé and cover letter will definitely help get the ball rolling. Also, while plain computer paper is okay to use, actual résumé paper is better because of its professional look and texture. Many students use regular printing paper, but you should use résumé paper for your résumé and cover letter.

In college, I went to the student center for assistance in preparing my résumé, and I noticed that pretty soon, everyone who went to the student center for help with their résumé often ended up with the same format, so there was no separation. At my college, this was one of the reasons why I constructed my résumé to my own liking, and pretty soon I was assisting others with their résumés as well. It always helps to get a personal opinion on your résumé from professors, counselors, and even peers because it will only make you stronger during your preparation stage for the career fair.

C. THE COLLEGE CAREER FAIR

When preparing for the career fair, always make sure that you allow yourself plenty of time to prepare and be ready, because this is considered an interview on your feet. While career fairs are normally used to allow different employers to explain what their companies do, most companies accept résumés and will often conduct a brief interview right there on-the-spot, so it pays to be prepared. Before you go to a career fair, the best thing to do is locate a list of specific employers that will be attending.

The list will include all the employers and their locations at the career fair to allow you to start preparing your résumés and cover letters. It's good to pick a few employers that you are interested in and start researching their companies, so when they ask if you've ever heard of them, you can give some type of description to break the ice. Have a few questions selected prior to the career fair so that you can communicate with the company representative instead of just standing there and listening.

When I went to my first career fair, I was very nervous. I was a sophomore in college trying to obtain an internship, so I figured I would start with the career fair. When I arrived, I was unorganized—I fumbled with my résumé because I was trying so hard to make a good impression, and the opposite was happening. I met with five different companies that I liked, and all of them told me to come back when I had more experience or was closer to graduation. I was completely crushed to hear that from the companies, because that was the last thing I expected to hear. I took that as a lesson, though, and I promised myself right then and there that I would do everything I could to stand out the next year so that I could be in a better position to obtain an internship.

If you look back at my career fair story, I pointed out that I was fumbling with papers, nervous, and had a lack of experience at the career fair and with the major employers. I struggled due to lack of preparation, and that's what I want you to avoid. I encourage you to start going to career fairs early on to become more comfortable and to watch everyone else and get a feel of what the environment is like. You certainly will have nothing to lose, and you will be stress free because nothing is expected and you're there out of curiosity. When I first went to the career fair, I took friends to make it seem less awkward that a sophomore was there, but after that first experience; I started going by myself and looking forward to each fair.

Since we covered making sure you are prepared documentation-wise, we will now discuss the proper attire to wear at the career fair. I highly advise not wearing jeans, shorts, flip-flops, or sneakers. The career fair is a place where you show representatives how professional you are, so you need to wear your best business formal attire. No matter where the career fair is located—whether it's in the gym, outside, or in the park—you wear your professional attire.

For the guys, that means suits and ties; for the ladies, that means either business suits or skirts that reach below or to the knees. If you're still having trouble figuring out what to wear, it's helpful to ask your professor, counselor, or student center, but your attire should be self-explanatory. If you don't have the financial means to obtain formal attire, please don't wait until the last minute to let someone know. If you don't have access to business attire, either borrow the attire from a friend or many student centers have clothes available for students to wear for interviews and career fairs. Those clothes are either bought or donated to the colleges by teachers or other students. Always make sure that you have the proper attire ready to go when it's time to introduce yourself to different companies at the fair.

To go along with your professional attire, carry a folder or padfolio to hold your résumés and any brochures or documentation that companies may give to you. Keep in mind that while it's great to have your résumés and cover letters with you, don't be offended if a company asks you to apply online. Some companies have different hiring protocols, so don't take it to heart if they don't immediately accept your résumé.

When you are through talking with each company, make sure you get the representatives' business cards and information so you can send them thank you letters. At the end of the day, a thank you letter could be the final ingredient that keeps you in the door. When I was in college, I attended a class where our guest speaker was an employee of a company that was well known to our major. When the representative stood in front of the class, she stated not to ever send a thank you letter to her, because that was cliché. She also advised not to follow up and to just be patient for a potential job interview to be set up on its own. Normally, I would take anyone's advice and make adjustments, but I disagreed with her—I felt that in order to show my appreciation for a representative taking the time to communicate with me, it should be followed with an innate sense of gratitude. That's why after she spoke with the class that day, I did what everyone was told not to do and sent her a thank you e-mail saying that regardless of how cliché it may be, I will always show respect and appreciation for anyone who gives advice on how to better myself.

She did respond with a short thanks, and I still ended up being given an interview. So, what I'm saying is to always follow up with some type of appreciation or thank you letter when speaking with a company, because that will take you far—trust me, it could result in you obtaining an interview or job.

D. FIRST INTERVIEW

Before an interview is even offered to you, you should have select times of when you would like to meet with employers. There are many ways in which companies communicate with you to set up interviews, including through phone, e-mail, in person, and even in a letter to your address. If you get a phone call and they ask you what time you would like to meet, never say whenever is convenient for them. They are trying to pursue you, so it pays to have an actual time and day of when you can meet. A mistake I made when a company called to schedule an interview was when they asked me when I would like to schedule the interview and I responded with whenever was convenient for them. During the initial conversation, they left by saying 'Well, we will get back to you,' and I said 'OK.' About two weeks passed before I realized what had happened and regretted not giving them a time to meet. That company could have very well have been busy or may have overlooked the calendar, but I took that as needing to let a company know when I would like to meet next time so that I could ensure my getting the interview.

Oftentimes, companies will have preselected times that you can select from for an interview. If that's the case, then choose the time they offer to you. If that time conflicts with a class, talk with your professor about it, because usually professors will excuse your absence. Some companies trying to meet with you may only have the time to communicate through e-mail for a potential interview. If this is the case, respond as quickly as possible with the same response as if you were getting a phone call. If they want to know what day to meet with you on, give them a date. Personally, when companies e-mailed me, it was less pressure for me to plan a meeting for a potential interview.

When I would get asked on the phone to set up a meeting, I felt unorganized because it was sort of at the spur of the moment; through email, though, I could take time to think about what date I wanted to give them, so it was much easier. The same responses when setting up an interview also goes for when they communicate with you in person or by a letter sent to your address—always have a suggested meeting time so you can easily move things along for the interview.

At least two days before your interview, make sure that you have enough accurate research on the company you're meeting with. If they have a website, browse around and look at some of the key things the company does. On their website, make sure to look at how well they did in the past and where they're trying to go in the future. You can often find reviews on the internet about the company as well as how much the employees like working there. Don't be deterred if you see negative reviews from company employees, because you don't know what role they played—they could be disgruntled employees that have a different opinion from others. Also keep in mind that this is just the start of your career, and if you love it at the company that selected you for the job, then stay there and continue to grow. If you don't like it, then realize that you are not obligated to stay there and thus you can continue your career someplace else. When you get a job at a company, remember that it doesn't have to be a lifelong commitment.

When the initial day of your interview comes, always arrive early. The appropriate time to arrive is between 15 and 30 minutes early. Whenever I had an interview, I would arrive 30 minutes early just to get a good sense of the environment and to calm myself in case I felt nervous. By arriving early, you rule out most errors, like not knowing where you're going or having vehicle trouble.

When I had interviews in Atlanta, I had to drive close to four hours to get there. The total number of hours spent on the road added up to eight hours round-trip. If I had a 1:00 p.m. interview in Atlanta, I was on the road at 7:00 a.m., because I didn't want there to be any mistakes in finding the location or with vehicle trouble, so I gave myself plenty of time. Those long drives took a physical and mental toll on me, so I typically arrived at the company two hours before my initial interview, which allowed me to rest and collect my thoughts. When you arrive, make sure you have your résumé and cover letter with you just in case your interviewer misplaced his or her copy or if you've updated it since the last time you all spoke or set up the interview.

When you meet the person you're interviewing with, make sure to smile when you greet them and let them know how thankful you are that they took the time to meet with you. Watch the way you position your body when you sit down in the interview area. Always sit up straight. Make eye contact with either that particular person or with everyone in the room when they address you. Speak slowly and clearly so that you're not potentially stuttering or stumbling over your words.

A neat trick I like to do whenever I'm in a room with more than three people is ask each person for a business card, and then stick them out in front of me according to where they sit at—that way, I will remember everyone's name. I've been in interviews where there was a round table of eight people staring at me, but I remained calm because I knew that everything on my résumé was the truth, and I felt comfortable because I knew what I was talking about. Since graduating from college, I've been in over 15 interviews, and I've learned something new each time. When the interviewer asks you a question, they look at your body language, your response, and how you sound when you give your response. Depending on what question you're asked, try to make sure it's not long or drawn out.

To save you from potentially dragging out a simple answer to a question like "So tell me about yourself," I always suggest that once you give your response, follow up with "Would you like me to elaborate more?" because it gives them the option to allow you to keep going or to continue with the interview process. When they do ask you a question like that, don't start off with the date you were born and what you did as a kid. It's good to mention where you grew up, how well you did in high school, and what made you choose your major; then move on to how active you were in college, and give some insight on your experiences that will be relevant to the position you are applying for. That's just a quick example of how to address that question. I highly recommend studying for your interview like you would a test.

When I had an interview, I would try to browse the internet for every question that could possibly be asked so I knew in advance how to address that question. The last thing you want to be caught doing is struggling on a simple question about something like your strengths or weaknesses. When they are explaining what the company does and what the job entails, always remain focused and make sure to listen perfectly. I've been on two interviews where employers quizzed me on what was previously discussed in the interview to see if I was paying close attention. It may sound weird, but there are interviewers out there who do that after an interview.

My favorite part of the interview is when they ask you whether you have any questions. It is imperative that you have questions prepared for them. When I first started interviewing for jobs, I wouldn't ask questions. However, I noticed that asking questions at least showed that I was interested in the position. The questions I loved to ask most were, What will my expectations be if I am selected for the position? What are some goals that your company and department want to meet? What are the odds that the job will have unexpected problems, because I want to be able to withstand anything that may come my way? Is this a new position that I'm interviewing for? What percentage will I be in a team setting versus by myself? Would it be possible to take a quick tour of the department?

These questions were shockers to employers because they are tailored to that specific position—you're secretly putting yourself in the role and suggesting that you've already been selected. Also, you get to discover more information that may not have been mentioned in the interview. In interviews, you'll likely be asked some behavior-based questions where they tell you to describe a time where you had to persevere or how you may have fixed a huge problem that came out of nowhere. When faced with questions like these, you should already have a story picked out for this situation. The best way to handle behavior-based questions is to explain the situation to the employer: how it arose, what problems you were facing, and how you corrected the problem and thus what you learned from the whole scenario.

The employer is trying to gauge how you act on your feet, so the more detailed and intricate the story is, the better perception they will have on how you may handle unexpected problems with this job. It's also okay to simply say you don't have an answer rather than just guessing at what you think it may be. There have been a few instances where I've been asked questions that I had no answer to, and I responded by simply saying, "At this moment I don't have an answer, but I know where to find out."

During interviews, you may be asked what your salary preference is. Before I answer this question, I should mention why I suggest the need for that particular salary figure. It depends on cost of living, expertise, what your major is worth, and the company that you are interviewing for. I wouldn't get too riled up in salary because if they want you, they will let you know what the job pays. The amount of experience and skills you possess will also be taken into account when they view the salary figure. Please keep in mind that when it comes to choosing a number, don't overdo it, but be realistic. I had a friend in college who didn't really do much but go to class and graduate—he didn't really stand out in college. When he went on his interview, he asked for $75,000, and the company laughed and said "Are you serious?" and he was dead serious. Unfortunately, he didn't get the call back for that position, and now that he has a job he sees why, so be optimistic but realistic.

With any interview, letters of recommendation can play a huge role. This goes back to the beginning when I spoke about establishing yourself early on and creating networks around you. Bringing letters of recommendation gives the employer an idea of what other people think about you. Don't just get a letter of recommendation from anybody like your grandma, sister, or someone you just met who offered to assist you. When it comes to letters of recommendation, past employers, college professors, and local community leaders can play a good role.

The best time to pull out your letters of recommendation is toward the end, so they can reflect after you leave on the people who are speaking about you. The letters of recommendation can also be considered your references. When writing down references to send to the interviewers, make sure you ask for their permission to be used as references. When the employers decide to call to get some information, you want them to be notified beforehand in order to eliminate any surprise or awkwardness that may occur. After the interview is over, make sure that you again thank the employers for taking the time with you and that you have everyone's e-mail contact. When you get back to your residence, send a thank you letter to the interviewers. The fact that you took the time to send them one more thank you is a very generous gesture.

The thank you letter is also another opportunity to remind the interviewer of why you should be selected for the position and how you will positively impact the company if you're selected. Once you have done all that you can, you just have to wait, but while waiting, continue learning and interviewing with other companies. If you sit and wait all day or week for one company to call, you will potentially turn into a nervous wreck and bring on a lot of unwanted stress, so continue forward. If the company does call and offer you the job and you decide that you want it, they will ask when you can start. This choice is up to you, but if you have to move to another state, town, or any location away from where you currently live, at least give yourself enough time to make the necessary adjustments. If a company doesn't call, don't take it to heart as if you interviewed very badly.

As I mentioned toward the beginning of this book, the job market is very competitive, so you will have competition. I guarantee you that you are not the only person applying for any one position. When I went to interviews that I didn't get called back on, I would continue learning and bettering myself to add more to my résumé so that I would stand out amongst everyone else. After each interview, I would also do a little self-assessment to see how well I did and if I minimized the mistakes that I may have made in prior interviews.

A lot of times after your interview, companies will be cordial enough to contact you regardless of whether they are offering you the job. They will either let you know that you didn't make it to the final round of interviews, tell you to come back for another interview, or even tell you to reapply for a different position within the company. There are also times when companies will not call you back at all, and while it may seem rude, you just have to accept reality—that's just the way some companies handle applicants, so never take offense to that.

E. FIRST DAY ON THE JOB

Assuming that you have now been offered the job and that you accepted it, you should approach it with a strong work ethic and open mind. If you will be part of a team, make sure you get to know everyone on that team, and learn how they work so you will know what to expect. When you start on day one, you will normally get a tour of your working environment and receive your tasks for that day. When you are given your first task, try to do your very best because it sort of sets the bar as to how your approach for future tasks will be.

Many jobs start you off with training, so take advantage of that time to show the employers how well and quickly you are able to master your training, and ask questions about anything that you don't understand so you can continue moving forward. On my first day of the job, I was very self-reliant and wanted to be the employee who only had to be told something once. I met my co-workers and spent a brief moment getting to know each of them and how they worked. I let them know up front that I looked forward to working with each and every one of them.

Get to work early on day one of your job to establish a great first impression of being good with time management. It's best to establish yourself as being self-reliant at the job, and that means not always needing someone to stand over you because you're afraid to make mistakes but trying to master things on your own first to make it easier on your boss—it will pay off in the long run. If you have to attend meetings, make sure you start taking great notes—bring a tape recorder if permitted because you want to have the eye for paying great attention to detail.

I carried a notepad everywhere I went at my first job, and I wrote down the names of anyone I met and what they did to establish them as a necessary contact if I needed information on certain things. Also, if you start taking good detailed notes, your boss may come back to you and even ask you about something that happened or was said in the meeting—that's another chance for you to show that you are organized and were paying attention.

Since I knew first off that I would be working with a team, I wanted to be the best team player. If anyone on my team needed assistance, I made sure I was there to assist. If someone on my team was going on vacation, I was always the first person to offer to cover for their time out of the office. Doing little things like that shows that you will do anything for the team because you want to see everyone grow and achieve to move to the next level in the business. That's the type of mentality corporations want to have inside their offices. I never stepped on anybody's toes because I had mental boundaries that I wouldn't cross—I knew that in order to be my best, I had to surround myself with the best, and what better way to be the best than to make sure nobody on my team fell behind? If you are in a position where you will have to give status updates on certain situations and inform people on how to do different tasks, establish yourself early on as a person of quick response.

For example, if someone e-mailed me wanting to know the status of something, I would quickly respond by saying "I'm looking into it right now" or "I will have you an answer in exactly two minutes." I never like to keep people guessing on when they will receive information from me because I never know what time frame they may be on, so I try to be as flexible as possible. When people start commending you on your good organization and quick responses, word travels fast—even to your boss—so you definitely want that reputation attached to your name. Keep in mind that this is how I conducted myself on the job since day one. I realize that everyone may have a different work pace than others, but how do you know how good you can be at something until you take the first step? Once I had that mentality, I loved stepping outside of my comfort zone to try new things.

If your job is dealing with customers who come into your office, you should want every customer to remember your name as well as the professionalism that you displayed. Remember, your reputation is what makes you who you are in the workplace. At work, keep an eye open for any opportunities that allow you the chance to establish yourself a better reputation. If your boss has some extra work that needs attention and nobody wants to be involved with it, there's your chance. There is always something that can be done to show that you thrive on working hard at your job. Start treating the work that other people hate to do like the work that you were born to do. Having this motive will separate you from everyone else.

When you enter any new work environment, a lot of employees may have their own personal opinions about other employees or even the way things should be done in the workplace. It's one thing for everybody to have their personal opinions, but it's another to let your personal opinions show in your work. When you are in the business environment, your personal opinions should stay to yourself. There will be times when you disagree with others around you, but there must be a platform of respect for both parties. If you disagree with someone and you feel very strongly about it, you should let them know—but in a respectful way to where they won't feel that you are trying to attack their ideas or actions. There will be times when you will meet the nicest people in the world, and there will also be times when you will meet the exact opposite. You will have to see and work with these people every day, so find some type of common ground and learn their way of doing thing before you show them your way, especially since you're new.

Whenever I walk out my door, however I felt that morning or the night before stays out of the workplace. I'm a very cheerful, ambitious, and positive person, and I want everyone to be comfortable and look forward to speaking with me. Things don't always go my way at work, but I look at it as there are 365 days in a year, so I'm entitled to a day where things don't go my way. I try to be the first person to greet everyone and ask how their day is going—it makes people feel good that you actually take the time to stop and ask them how they are doing.

A lot of people don't really socialize at all at work and end up feeling like an outlier. My perception of work is that you want to get everything that's important taken care of, but you want to have fun as well. I find that it's easy for a person to find enjoyment in the work they love to do. If you are perhaps in a career that you had to take to make ends meet, then you should treat it like you love it—a not-so-positive mentality will begin to show after a while, and you don't want that. I always suggest continuing working on getting into the career of your dreams while working in another career at the same time.

A lot of companies have different types of organizations within their network that are for employees to join and participate in. I highly suggest getting started with one of these organizations. When you join one of the organizations, networking will be easy because people will approach you to instantly connect with you. The people you meet within the organization of your choosing can benefit your career significantly. I've been a member of several organizations in my career, and everyone I've met has given me personal advice for advancing my career. I was introduced to people who had the ability to elaborate more on the different sides of the company that I worked for and who gave me their personal opinions on different things.

F. CONTINUED SELF-GROWTH

Once you have gained more confidence at work, you want to keep the routine going. The word "consistency" is what you should display in your life and work environment. The more consistent you are, the more people will be reassured of your abilities. Whether you're a great supportive employee or self-motivated employee, you have to be consistent. In the workplace, you only get one chance to make a first impression, and after that, you must continue to grow and better yourself. I am a huge supporter of the mentality of growing as a person each and every day.

In the workplace, just like in college and in life, you have to be self-reliant or you won't get far. It's important to be able to motivate yourself through hard times and good times. While you may have supportive co-workers, family, and friends around you, eventually you have to find the strength and power from inside you and depend on yourself to get to where you want to be.

One thing that I do to motivate myself is post quotes that I make up each morning. The reason I post my own made-up quotes and not anyone else's is because it puts my brain into a creative mode each day. Whenever my day isn't going as planned, I look at the quote I put up for that day as a reminder to be resilient and to remember that I can overcome any challenges that come my way. This advice applies to both the young and older generations.

There is a place inside each of us that holds all our dreams and aspirations, and sometimes we think it may be too late, or we lose sight of it or simply give up on it. Those same dreams and aspirations will always be there waiting for you to take that first step toward them. If you're inside the workplace and you want to be a director in a few years, set your mind to it, work out a plan, and then follow through with it. It's that simple. If you want to receive a certain certification, then research it and all the criteria that it will take to accomplish it, schedule time to prepare for it, and set your mind to focusing on what you want to achieve—you can do it.

I have sort of a lock in mentality. Before I wrote this book, I was trying to do five things at the same time, and I could never prioritize the tasks I wanted to complete first. My mindset was that if I tried to work a little on each of my goals at the same time, then I could accomplish them all together at the same time. I found out that it would take me even longer to complete tasks had I continued to do things like that. What I decided to do instead was start locking in on what I wanted to achieve, task by task, and I started completing things more quickly and thus built my confidence even more. If you set both short-term and long-term goals, completing your short-term goals will keep you motivated to want to continue forward with your long-term goals.

For example, when I was in college and went to the career fair, I listened to what company representatives told me I needed to do to catch their eye, went back to the school, and started right then and there to come up with ways to better myself so that I could be a high commodity at the next career fair. When I went back to the career fair, I received an interview from every company that I gave my resume and applied for. When I put in the effort to get the results I wanted and ended up achieving those results, a light came on inside of me that reminded me of what you put into something is what you get out of it, and I continued that approach all the way into my career.

After I graduated from college, I knew I had to keep learning because the world was changing each and every day. Especially since my major dealt with technology, I knew I had to keep up with the latest news. I enabled myself to grow by becoming more aware of what was going on around me. I started paying more attention to the way I articulated my point of views and speech, the way I received information, and the way I conducted myself on a daily bases.

Every day, I found a new way to better myself. I stayed hungry for knowledge and made sure I conversed with directors and experienced co-workers frequently so that they could help steer me in the direction that I wanted to go. While all these are great examples of how I grew as a person, I knew that a majority of the work that it took to get me to where I am now all started with me wanting to be successful in life.

Growing as a person starts within you. I know I make it sound easy, but it wasn't for me, and it won't be for you. I literally had to break out of some habits that I was too comfortable with. I came into college with a "just do enough to get by" approach and saw how far that got me—I knew I needed to work hard. If you're trying to change habits that you have been comfortable with for years, it is definitely going to take some work. Before I could change, I had to take a long, hard look at myself and first let myself know why I needed to change. I needed to change because I knew that my old habits and mindset were only going to get me so far in life. I first started dreaming more then I normally did because I had to see where I wanted to go in order to discipline myself to get there. Next I had to make sure that I wouldn't let anything get in the way of reaching my goals. Being young and from a small town, my role models were my parents, world leaders, and activists. Nobody the town knew had actually gone out and made it big in the corporate world or beyond. Since I knew this, I automatically set my first goal to be the first.

Once I had that down, I knew that I had to withdraw myself from distractions that would hinder me from achieving my goals—such as being involved with friends whose goals weren't as strong as mine—and just start depending on myself for motivation. I started looking at my father as well as different famous entrepreneurs, political figures, college professors, and counselors as my role models to sort of develop a blueprint for the type of person I wanted to become. I studied these people like textbooks because I knew that being like people of that stature could only help get me to where I wanted to go. Through all this, I began to grow mentally, emotionally, and spiritually. I knew that all those men and women had one thing in common: they had confidence in themselves. I had to gain confidence for myself because my dreams would just be dreams otherwise. I gained confidence by beginning to know who I was as a person and becoming sure of myself. Those men and women I looked up to had fears, but they didn't let those fears deter them from getting to where they needed to be and doing what needed to be done.

At a young age, I wanted to be this fearless individual who easily stood out everywhere I went. I wanted to be very vocal, resilient, energetic, positive, ambitious, and creative. Those were all the qualities that I wanted to be my platform for success. When you're setting goals, it pays to consistently remind yourself of your mission in working toward your goals. The more you see your goals and say that you can accomplish them, the more your conscious mind works toward them—and your subconscious mind will follow suit as well. To be more specific, your subconscious mind is just your brain reacting to repetitive tasks that have already been done.

For example, when writing your name, you've done it so much that you can write it without even thinking about it. If you want to succeed in something, keep reminding yourself of how much you want it, and your subconscious mind will be programmed to allow you to go through anything to achieve your goals. There are many things that I want to achieve in my life, and there are also instances when I will get distracted from my goals. To stay focused, I've consistently played out my goals and successes so much that a mental switch will trigger me whenever I'm distracted for a long amount of time.

Another thing about self-growth that some of us tend to forget is introducing ourselves to new areas and cultures. It's not always good to stay in one particular area for a long amount of time because the need for something to look forward to will start withering away. When you travel, you get to feel the unexpected, and it's an adventure that fulfills your self-growth. After I graduated from college and a few weeks before I started my career, I saved money and left the state whenever I had the chance. With a small budget, I travelled up and down the east coast, experiencing the different areas and the fast cities that took pride in the structures and reputations they had built. For a kid from a small town, going to different states was very big for me, especially compared to other students who were fortunate enough to travel abroad. I knew for a fact that there was a whole new world out there waiting for me, and that pushed me even more to work hard because I wanted to go see it.

When I was in college, I had many friends who were from different countries and different backgrounds, and they would share stories of what it was like to live in their countries. Sitting with my friends and listening to them tell me about some of the great times as well as the struggles they had to overcome to get to America was like a wake-up call for me. They saw me as being in a good position, when I thought at times that the odds were not in my favor. Their ability to work so hard to come over from their country to America, master their studies, and start businesses and careers was mind-blowing to me.

From college to being in the corporate world now, I'm dealing with those same people from those different cultures, and their mindset along with mine is even more focused. It was never about who was better, smarter, or stronger, it was about setting your mind to achieve something and then going to get it. When I couldn't see the world, I listened to their stories and got a change of perspective outside of where I had been living my whole life. That was my self-growth right there. Since being out of college, I have been fortunate enough to have the opportunity to start travelling abroad, and I must say that the feeling of having options on the table is impeccable. A lot of companies that you will be working for may require you to travel, and I say go for it. Remember that there is a whole world out there for you to see, and if you restrain yourself from seeing it, you'll be losing out on some of the most rewarding benefits. The last thing I want to leave you with is to stay focused, persevere, and never let anything stop you from becoming the person you want to be.

CHECK OUT THE WEBSITE FOR MORE INFORMATION
WWW.MAKINGMOVESINCOLLEGE.COM